From

Six migrant stories

Anne Henderson

ALLEN & UNWIN

for Elizabeth and Johannah

First published 1993
Allen & Unwin Pty Ltd
9 Atchison Street, St Leonards, NSW 2065 Australia

National Library of Australia
Cataloguing-in-Publication entry:

Henderson, Anne, 1949-
    From all corners: six migrant stories

    ISBN 1 86373 510 0

    1. Women immigrants—Australia—Case studies.
    2. Australia—Emigration and immigration—
    Case studies. I. Title

305.48800994

Set in 11/12½ Garamond by DOCUPRO, Sydney
Printed by Southwood Press, Marrickville

Contents

Acknowledgements

M any thanks to Lily, who unknowingly gave me the idea for this book, and to Rita, Judy, Lilah, Nhung and Phi and their families for allowing me to retell their stories. A particular thanks also to the Carmelite community at Kew in Melbourne for allowing me to visit as and when necessary, and for the many afternoon teas.

For the chapter 'Judy' I am indebted to Sister Carmel Leavey of the Dominican Order and Sister Rose Macginley of the Presentation Order, for their help with the historical detail relating to the Dominicans in Australia. Sister Carmel Leavey also provided useful material compiled in the *National Statistical Survey of Religious Personnel: Australia—1976* and *Reflections on a Survey: Australian Religious Personnel 1978* (available from the Institute of Religious Studies, NSW).

I am grateful to Lalita Mathias for her excellent work typing the interview transcripts and for other technical assistance, to Astrid Riley for help with the mysteries of the Word Perfect 5.0 system and to Rachel Fairfax who drew the maps. Also to my daughters Elizabeth and Johannah for proof reading and general remarks and to Anne Vipond and Veronica Henderson who read the final draft. In the background, for consultation on family memorabilia and other details, my mother, Gwen, and Alice Ironside were invaluable.

For support, encouragement and helpful suggestions on the text, a special thanks to my husband Gerard; above all for never saying, 'You'll never finish it'.

Beginnings

Some say Australia is losing its way, becoming confused about national identity. They draw wistful views of an earlier Australia—an harmonious Anglophile colony with mono beliefs and uniform cultural heritage. 'Separate' development, they argue, is un-Australian. Whenever I hear all of this I am puzzled. Looking back I see a different picture.

Australia for me has always been multicultural. Before I was born my second generation Catholic Irish father, from Brunswick in Melbourne, started the process by marrying my mother, recently converted to Catholicism from a Protestant background as the daughter of an Englishman from Yorkshire and a woman of mixed Scottish and Danish origins. We grew up with the Protestant cousins on one side and the Catholics on the other. But for a long time we were closer to the children of my mother's Anglo-Celt bridesmaid, who married an Italian and made the words 'Genoa Terrazzo' standard in the family vocabulary. When I became my parents' bundle of bouncing joy just one month before Robert Menzies won the 1949 election, the years of postwar immigration from Europe were warming up. Not long after, my father's friend and singing companion, Gladys, as Australian as hot tea, married Stefan from Poland.

But the plot thickened. By the time I had a sister and a brother, we had moved from Clifton Hill to the outskirts of Donvale to live a semi-rustic existence four miles from the nearest railway station at Mitcham, where my father caught the train to work in the city each day. For a while we had no car. A fan of Banjo Paterson, Henry Lawson, C.J. Dennis, Ion Idriess and Teilhard de Chardin my father was something of a romantic. He was also a staunch Catholic. The nearest

1

church was at the Monastery run by Carmelite priests two miles away, a walk we often made in order to attend Mass on Sundays. Mass was at 6 am. It was a nature walk we hardly appreciated at the time, through natural bush scented with gum, pine and wattle, thick over the dirt road, policed by magpies and serenaded by bell birds. We passed the Pellegrinos' small farm as we emerged into the orchards of Donvale and said good morning to the Monastery cows who passed us on the track returning from the milking sheds to their lower level pasture, now the site of a large boys' college. But the early morning Australian idyll ended at the chapel door, where at Mass for the next half an hour every word spoken was in Latin. There were no sermons.

In our rural setting, so removed from urban and cosmopolitan influences, there was much cultural difference. Joe and Anna Tittoto at the top of the hill gave me my first contact with real Italian food. I had to eat a huge bowl of spaghetti with meat sauce—and the main meal hadn't started. Joe grew succulent asparagus in his garden long before it was sold fresh by most Australian fruiterers. Betty Flisowski, who had hidden her husband during the war somewhere in Poland, first from the Nazis and then from the Red Army, introduced us to the smell of strong European cigarettes and a thousand foreign tastes. In her thick guttural English she told us stories and petted and spoiled us with little treats. And she introduced the whole family to the edibility of new sorts of mushrooms which Australians thought were poisonous. We harvested loads of these large fungi found on the thick needle floors of the local pine forests which were our playground. Betty pickled them in bottles and fried them in oil, and we ate them. One kind was large and orange with a circle of delicate sandy-coloured frills underneath; the other was a slimy brown with a bright yellow underbelly. Our Australian relatives thought we had become very bohemian. And then there was old Bill Domeney, retired officer class, and his wife, both as Anglophile as the Indian colonial service. Bill's wife served exotic pungently smelling teas in her chintz-covered sitting room. Bill drove his FJ Holden car very slowly and dressed with tweedy country style. His garden was full of olde worlde shrubs and tended lovingly.

A year or two after learning to walk my sister and I

attended our first lessons. They were Irish dancing classes held in the parish hall at Clifton Hill. By the time we started real school our parish primary was in Mitcham. The school bus also picked up children from the local State school and for the first few years we spent much of the time on board breaking down demarcation lines between the different school cultures. We Catholics could fascinate the State school girls with rosary beads and holy medals which they seemed to regard as pieces of pretty jewellery. One afternoon I nearly made a convert by promising to give my Mary medal to a small girl from the State school.

The postwar boom in immigration to Australia affected one institution more than any other: it had an enormous impact on the Catholic Church. The Irish-dominated religion I was born into would dissipate as I grew up. In 1980 Lidio Bertelli, assistant director of the Melbourne Catholic Intercultural Resource Centre, called attention to this change saying, 'It is right to call this archdiocese an immigrant church'.[1] Figures released at the time showed that migrants from southern Europe numbered 200 000 in the Melbourne archdiocese and that 29 per cent of Victorian Catholics were born overseas while the national proportion was a much lower 24 per cent. It was much the same story in most other states.

At school in the 1950s the cultural influx was certainly apparent at the parish school in Mitcham. The school's catchment area included the suburb of Nunawading where the government hostel for newly arrived immigrants was located. Many of the children went through the Mitcham parish school, in the firm control of the sisters of St Joseph, champions of the underprivileged and even then praying that their founder, Mary McKillop, would become Australia's first saint. The Dutch who came in large numbers had little English. Quick readers among the Australian students were given small groups which they helped, sitting on the floor under the blackboard. My best friend was Dalia from Lithuania, with a sister called Raza and a brother called Alge. Our Australian vocabulary was expanding. At Dalia's house her parents spoke quite good English but they often chatted together in their native Lithuanian during meals. I got used to sitting with people talking in a language I did not understand and soon it seemed natural. As life moved on I often found myself in homes where parents spoke to one another in a foreign language. We heard stories from everywhere: about the war, about hiding from the Germans and hiding from the Russians, about life in Europe; the cramped voyages of assisted passages; what it was like to stop at Port Said and to go through the Suez Canal. They added another dimension to our home's family folklore which offered stories like that of great-grandfather John, who studied briefly for the priesthood at Maynooth near Dublin, was rejected by his family in Cork when he left, so came to Australia. And great-grandmother Mary, on the other side, who left Scotland in the 1880s with her brother to travel first to Melbourne and then on alone to northern Queensland where she found work as a dairy maid. Above all they contrasted strangely with the stories we fed on at home from old books found in odd corners. We read the very English 1914 edition of *The Progress To Literature* series from my mother's childhood, school prize books such as a biography of Robert Burns presented in 1899 to grandfather's cousin Arthur 'For Punctual Attendance and Good Conduct' at the Elland Upper Edge Baptist Sunday school, and Kipling's *Puck of Pook's Hill* presented for 'Geography' at a Queensland high school which my mother attended in 1939.

In 1954 the new young English Queen Elizabeth II came to visit Australia with her good-looking husband Philip. Melbourne streets shone with thousands of lights and decorative crowns and emblems in a host of light bulbs. We waited kerbside with thousands of others to wave little flags that looked like Union Jacks at these dazzling figures of importance and I boasted to friends that I had seen Her Majesty four times. But it was the celebrity status that drew our attendance, not wide-eyed Empire loyalty. Our Irish great-grandfather had passed on the message that for generations the English had dispossessed the tenant farmers among his family and neighbours. And my father had left us in no doubt that Winston Churchill had deserted Australia when Singapore fell to the Japanese in World War II. Years later a reading of history suggested both attitudes were a little one-sided but at home in 1954 they held sway. As the Queen passed we watched with the sort of need-to-be-there that many non-

Catholic politicians displayed in 1986, lining up in Kings Hall, Canberra, eager to meet the celebrity Pope John Paul II. Growing up in Australia as a Catholic was to grow up in an enclave constantly invaded by other enclaves. Our Catholic education system was the triumph of prelates like Archbishop Daniel Mannix of Melbourne and Archbishop Michael Kelly of Sydney, who built up a separate system of schooling under the umbrella of the Catholic archdioceses and dioceses. Parents paid small sums, like two shillings and sixpence a week for each child, so that a few lay teachers could be employed to add to the majority force of nuns. At secondary school there were modest fees. The curriculum included large dollops of Christian Doctrine alongside the regular, often inspected, State Education Department syllabus.

Our Catholic separate development, watched over by the careful eye of the State, had started in the wake of the Education Acts of the colonies, beginning with South Australia in 1851 and ending with Victoria in 1872, which had made education free, secular and compulsory, bringing to an end Australia's long colonial period of government-sponsored multiculturalism. It was a victory, albeit temporary, for the mono-culturalists.

The early practice of multiculturalism involved government handouts to the religious denominations of the colonies for the purpose of educating, entirely free of government interference, children belonging to the different church groups. Since the churches largely split up along ethnic lines, Irish, Scottish and English, this represented a cultural as well as religious segmentation. Small Jewish communities also found sponsorship under this policy. Resistance by the Catholic bishops to the mono-cultural prescriptions of the secularists and the Education Acts eventually ensured the mushrooming of parish church schools funded by their Catholic communities. When State Aid to non-government schools began in 1963 the white flag went up for the mono-culturalists although they had long before lost the battle.

When I was born Australia had been denied the experience of a noticeable Asian component in its immigrant melting pot for nearly half a century. The White Australia Policy had ensured the exclusion of non-Europeans, except in the narrowest of circumstances. Non-Brits were also not encouraged and it was hoped that Australia would mirror the societies of England, Scotland, Wales and Ireland which had claimed the southern continent in 1788. But by 1939 a growing number had found their way in from Italy, Germany and Greece to nibble at the edges of Anglo-Celt society.

In the decades after 1950 the forces of a new style immigration program of assisted immigrants from non-British Europe began to change the protected bastion I had screamed my way into at Mena House maternity hospital, East Melbourne. By the time I returned to the environs of a labour ward in 1973 to have my first child, the nurseries of most local hospitals had witnessed a quiet revolution. Of the more than two million new Australians to take up residence in those years, only 42 per cent were from Britain. Nearly all the rest were from northern, eastern and southern Europe. With the gradual relaxing of the White Australia Policy in the 1960s and its formal demise in 1973, the following decades added to the complexity of the ethnic mix. After 1976, the Fraser Government initiated the first real test of the new non-discriminatory immigration policy by accepting large numbers of Vietnamese boat people following the massive exodus of refugees from Communist Vietnam which made their plight a world concern. In the maternity wards the little heads continued to get darker.

'By 1975', writes James Jupp in his study *Immigration*, 'the non-British component of Australian society had become too large to be ignored'.[2] Following the Galbally Report in 1978,[3] government-sponsored programs to assist diverse ethnic and cultural groups began. Before long a debate over national identity was under way.

In July 1980 Professor Lauchlan Chipman wrote to *The Australian* to protest at the Australian Government's commitment to spending on a Multicultural Broadcasting Service (later to be called SBS).[4] He was an early voice in what was soon a crescendo of wails about 'multiculturalism'. On talkback radio, in the print media, on television, in parliaments and in homes the topic was an obsession throughout the 1980s. At times it seemed as if the deletion of a single word from the Australian vocabulary would overnight transform all ills into success. If Australia did not have 'multiculturalism' the dollar would rise, interest rates fall, inflation disappear, recessions would end, the balance of payments problems would be solved and there would be more goodies for everyone. Never has there been such a scapegoat.

Writing in *The Long Journey: Vietnamese Migration and Settlement in Australia* in 1984, Dr Nancy Viviani argued that the mindset that accepted the White Australia Policy for so long in Australia's history was only living underground and not completely gone. Later that year Professor Geoffrey Blainey began a debate on what the right sort of composition for the Australian population should be, and went on to single out Asian immigrants to Australia as one group which should not be allowed to increase as naturally as others. In 1984 Asian immigrants made up less than 5 per cent of the Australian population but their proportion among new immigrants was more like 40 per cent. Professor Blainey also railed against multiculturalism as the arm of the open door policy on immigration.

For a time the simmering racial discussion which this unleashed suggested that Nancy Viviani was on to something. Opinion polls began reporting that a majority of Australians were against either immigration or Asian immigration. In quick succession Liberal politicians, beginning with Michael Hodgman of Tasmania and continuing with John Howard as Liberal leader in 1988 and John Hewson in 1990, tried to exploit these polls arguing various cases against multiculturalism and immigration. On the other side of politics the ALP member for Kalgoorlie, English-born Graeme Campbell, embarrassed his colleagues by uttering dire predictions in May 1991 that racial riots in Australia would soon break out. His evidence in support of his claim was the riots of Britain's Brixton and he went on from this to assert that multiculturalism had not been good for Australia. In 1992 Mr Campbell openly called for a return of the White Australia Policy.

For some the debate over multiculturalism was about the allocation of government money. For others it became a side door into a public expression of bigotry directed against different racial groups entering Australia as immigrants. It is the kind of bigotry which Australian journalist Gregory Hywood, writing in *The Australian Financial Review* in 1988 from the United States, described as unacceptable in America.

The United States, said Mr Hywood, does not 'debate rights in terms of race. The last time it did—in the 1960s—cities burned, literally'.[5] This was true.

In Australia, however, cities did not burn and there were no race riots from a debate couched in racial terms, even in bigoted ones. Instead John Howard's popularity took a dive when he refused to withdraw comments that Asian migration to Australia should be slowed down. Increasingly the debate over multiculturalism tended to become a debate over immigration. And eventually immigration lost. By the end of 1992 official attitudes to refugees in internment in Australia were inclined to favour sending them back. Moreover, new immigrant numbers had been reduced in the platforms of both government and opposition parties, and the 20 000 Chinese students given temporary residence in Australia after the 1989 Tienanmen Square massacre were facing still more doubt about their status in spite of government assurances from time to time that they could stay.

But a slowdown in immigration will only slow population change. It will not bring back what was. Today more than 40 per cent of Australians are overseas-born or have parents born overseas. Australia now is home for people from 130 different nations. A future Liberal–National Coalition Government might try to remove the word 'multiculturalism' from all government documents. But that will have little impact on multicultural Australia. It is here to stay.

The Chinese American writer Maxine Hong Kingston has said that 'in order to tell the story of Australia or America— countries where people of all nationalities meet—you have to tell the story of the world'.[6] In her vision we are all citizens of the world. She sees herself as one kind of American and every American as multicultural, deriving different bits of America from different kinds of American experience available from various cultural outlets. She says she is black because she knows a lot of blacks, white because she studied white history. She applies the same philosophy to Australia or any country where a variety of ethnic and cultural experiences are available.

Over the years I have had many contacts with Maxine Hong Kingston's vision of different kinds of Australian. In 1992 I singled out six of them because they are especially different and recorded each of their experiences of becoming Australian. As I boarded the plane at Sydney airport in late June to start the project, heading for Melbourne, the unemployment figures had been hovering around 10 per cent for months (worse was to come) and scapegoating was becoming a national sport. A cry of 'no English, no ticket, no start' was once more taking vogue as a way to cull the immigrant intake and the Aussie battler was riding high as victim. Global villagers weren't welcome.

Rita, Lily, Judy, Lilah, Nhung and Phi have birthdates that span more than half a century. Each chose to come to Australia as a single woman leaving a family behind. Only one spoke English before starting out. Each defied the odds by coming to Australia. Three of them risked their lives, one risked imprisonment. As immigrant Australians they faced difficult and at times seemingly insurmountable hurdles.

In appreciating the complexity of the Australian identity these friends are an important ingredient. Taken as a whole their stories intersect with Australian history and unfold as part of a national drama taking place between the 1930s and the present day. Taken individually they display most of the important elements in Australia's story as a nation of successful settlement. Above all they are a reminder of the value and richness of diversity and difference in national cohesion.

Rita

Tнᴇ question on my mind was would she do it? Or was it too late for recollections? Rita had gone quiet with others. So I arrived not knowing what she would say. As it turned out it wasn't a problem and for nearly an hour we zig-zagged about, fitting things together with jabs of memory, going back and forward in time, tracing a gutsy, ironic and familiar pattern.

Rita told me her story when she was 87. We sat in her architect-designed home in Kew, one of Melbourne's eastern suburbs. Rita's youngest daughter, Anna, joined us and helped with bits and pieces, threading together time and place and playing interpreter. Isabella, Rita's eldest daughter, was not far from the action either. She was in Palermo, Sicily, for a wedding.

I have known them for more than twenty-five years, Rita, Anna, Mirella and Isabella. Their home, a unique femocracy (dogs Nero I & II have been males), is a favourite drop-by place. At its centre is Rita, a little slower now, her round strong figure of the Mediterranean mama topped with softly shaped white hair. She is always just a step or two behind Anna or Isabella at the front door, usually emerging from the kitchen, laughing a cackle of welcome while we all talk at once, asking 'How is your family?' in her familiar Italian English.

While Rita told her story we sat at the family room table, photos of relatives in Italy and Australia at arm's reach on the wall unit behind me. Anna's pasta sauce warmed on the benchtop stove and some winter sunshine brightened the polished timber floor through full length casement windows. Sunday afternoon in the street outside was sleepy and suburban.

Like those arriving in the troubled 1990s, Rita came to Australia at a time of high unemployment when the depression of the 1930s could still be felt in the dole queues and sustenance work programs which lasted for nearly a decade. At the time there were many who argued that newcomers like Rita were bad news, taking the jobs of needy Australians and adding to the unemployment figures simultaneously. The rational mind would say it was impossible to do both. In the event Rita did neither.

Tape recorder on, we hit the plot midpoint with Rita's opening line: *I'd never been to school after I came back from the war.*

The war was World War I. Rita had begun her story in 1916 when her home in Tarcento, in Friuli, Italy, had become a war zone. The twelve year old and her family had been forced along with the flow of refugees, fleeing as the Germans moved south following the notorious Battle of Caporetto which broke the Italian advance near the Austrian border. Italy had only just entered the war.

In *A Farewell To Arms* Ernest Hemingway records the scene when his hero encounters a column of refugees in carts laden with their household valuables on the road outside the town of Udine. The novelist sketched them after taking research notes from military records and you can find what he wrote on page 143 of the modern Grafton paperback. They are described as just one more obstacle in the midst of

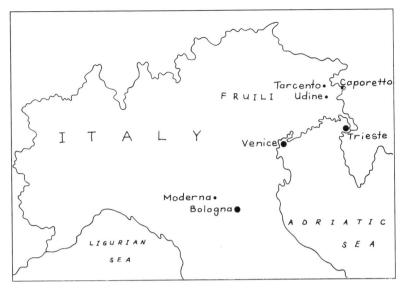

a muddy retreat. Somewhere among Hemingway's fictional moving mass of displaced humanity was the real Rita and her relatives.

Outside Modena, 250 kilometres to the south near Bologna, Rita's family found temporary shelter with about twenty other families. They made most of the journey by train. At Nonantola they were cared for in the grounds of a grand estate converted into a refugee centre. Here the one teacher struggled to pacify a crowd of youngsters. Rita shrugs at the thought of her schooling there.

There was a bit of school. Not much. They were mixed—big and small. The teacher made us play to keep us out of trouble for the mothers. She read poetry or something. That's all. There was only one teacher. She couldn't teach everybody. Afterwards my big brother wanted to make me go to school. I should have gone to school till I was fourteen or fifteen. That was the law.

When the Germans were turned back within the year the family returned to Tarcento. In the village Rita stayed at home helping her mother. She was the youngest of six children. Soon after the end of the war Rita's father, who was a shoemaker, died leaving the older children to find what work they could to help support the family.

Tarcento is a settlement in the foothills south east of the

Dolomites, a hybrid zone between the Venetian plain and the Alpine border with Austria. It is just a few kilometres from where Benito Mussolini was a schoolteacher in 1907 when his students nicknamed him 'the tyrant'. Looked down on Tarcento is a cluster of terracotta roofing surrounded by green wooded hills and farmlands. Mulberry and cherry trees dominate the landscape. It is no scorched Mediterranean vista. At easy distances to the south of Tarcento are Trieste and Venice.

In the larger towns of Friuli modern industrial development is today a feature of everyday life and in the smaller towns modern conveniences are everywhere. Village life for Rita, however, offered few luxuries. *I had to stay home with my mother—cooking, washing, getting the water outside because there were no taps. Now they have everything, just like here and maybe more. Then it was different.*

A dressmaker who worked for Rita's mother taught her to sew. At first there were no formal lessons. The child picked up the trade with the pins from the floor. By fourteen she and her older sister, Elisa, were learning professionally. *My mother had a good girl dressmaker who worked in business with her mother. Before we ran away during the war I joined them after school to make a little bit of stitching. At fourteen I actually started to learn dressmaking with them. My sister too.*

The sisters developed easily as tailors. They could flip through magazines and adapt new lines, drafting patterns for styles just coming into vogue. Before long they had gone into business for themselves, producing garments of high couture. In 1934 they were employing about twenty women. By that time Benito Mussolini had been Italy's dictator for ten years. When he and his entourage had swept through Tarcento a few years earlier Rita and Elisa were contracted to make hundreds of little flags for the townsfolk to wave in Mussolini's honour.

For the average Australian the Fascist dictator Benito Mussolini is just one of the many big names of the 1930s. He is seen in old newsreels waving his arms about and haranguing the Italian masses. A few older Italian Australians still harbour a respect for the man who made Italy strong on the world stage when they and their families were so poor. But for Rita and her sister, Mussolini's greater public spending meant there were higher and higher taxes to pay. *I built up a business and then they started to bring in all these regulations. The usual thing. We were working hard, like right through the night sometimes, to get things done. We would get paid. But not enough to pay all those taxes.*

Italy was experiencing a period of Fascist government. Its ruler, Mussolini (Il Duce), had made himself a dictator shortly after becoming Prime Minister in 1922. He ruled with arbitrary force in a divide-and-conquer style. Local governments were no longer elected and instead were run by centrally appointed officials answerable to Il Duce. Each mayor competed for power with one other centrally appointed political figure, the Party Secretary. Mussolini had begun life as a socialist. As a Fascist, his approach to economics continued much of the socialist fervour for big government spending and high taxation. Italy's senior bureaucracy was expanded with favoured appointees on high salaries. The economy groaned under the weight of a new costly burden. And Mussolini's ego needed a lot of stroking, so the lira was protected from devaluation, although for some time it fell anyway. Exporters lost money, share values fell, unemployment rose as did the cost of production. Italian wheat was protected by placing high tariffs on imported wheat which forced up the cost of basic foodstuffs. Mussolini wrote a poem on wheat.

In the early years of Mussolini's Italy when the economy deteriorated, Rita's brother, Albano, chose emigration. As a Friulian he was tracing a familiar pattern—emigration is in the blood. From their agricultural economy the search for buyers in the trading of wares had taken Friulian menfolk to other Italian centres for decades. The building tradesmen had followed, moving out into other parts of Europe and then eventually into the newer continents of the Americas and Australia. From such pioneers networks developed relaying back to fellow Friulians information on the prospects to be found, good or bad, in these far flung settlements.

In 1926 Albano headed for Australia where the opportunities were much better. He was not to know that in 1929 Australia would join the world in a great depression and that he would have to battle to find work and maintain a living so far from home. Still, that is what happened and Albano

went on to become the link in the migration chain for his
sisters.

   With the Nazis' victory in Germany in 1933 there was an
informal alliance between Hitler's Germany and Fascist Italy.
Germany encouraged Mussolini to become the dominant
power in North Africa to displace the French, a sound tactical
move for Germany and one that appealed to Mussolini's
vanity. In 1935 Mussolini embarked on his ambitious plan to
invade Abyssinia. Through September his aggressive campaign filled the headlines of daily newspapers around the
world. By October the offensive had begun. In Tarcento Rita's
family began to encourage her and Elisa to leave. Even *The
Age* in Melbourne carried headlines that war was inevitable.
Rita remembers the mood of the time.

There was the war in Abyssinia; it had just started.
Albano was back in Melbourne. He said it was getting
better and if we liked to come there he would sponsor us.
Maybe in two or three years we would come back because
my mother was still by herself. My married brother, who
was the first in the family, was in a wine business with a
restaurant. My mother was very happy to go with him. I
don't know what papers we needed to have. Albano
arranged it all. The passports were fixed. Everybody say
we've got to go. There is a war on.

   Rita was thirty. Elisa was just a bit older. They spoke no
English but this did not discourage them from booking passages on the English ship *Orion* of the Orient Line which was
making its maiden voyage. They embarked in Naples. With
them they took their sewing machine, packed into a large
trunk to be loaded onto the ship. Three days before they left,
on 3 October 1935, Italy began bombing Adowa in Ethiopia.
In Melbourne, their destination, Collingwood won its tenth
football premiership by defeating South Melbourne.

   The trip to Australia took exactly a month. In the Mediterranean the passengers of the *Orion* heard and saw nothing
of the international incidents surrounding their route. On
board Rita and Elisa got around the limits of language with
the help of the ship's purser. A souvenir menu from the
'Landfall Dinner', held just before they arrived in Melbourne,
suggests that the two Italian passengers from Tarcento had

managed to communicate very well. The menu, kept from the dinner, was signed by passengers from around the world, about twenty names in all, including a Galbally from Melbourne. Rita remembers one passenger especially—a jockey from England heading for the Victorian spring racing carnival.

The *Orion*'s arrival at Station Pier, Port Melbourne, on Cup Eve was widely reported in the press and preparations were begun for a gala ball on board to celebrate its first visit to Melbourne. Passengers included Sir Henry Gullett, coming back from an Empire delegation visit, and Lady Walder and her daughter, returning from the wedding in England of Philip Game, son of the former Governor of New South Wales. The social pages do not record, however, the arrival of Rita or the jockey. The next day the favourite Marabou won the Melbourne Cup, ridden by a former New Zealander. A day later the future Governor-General of Australia, the Duke of Gloucester, married Lady Alice Scott in a private chapel at Buckingham Palace and Billy Hughes split yet again from the Cabinet, resigning this time from the government of Joseph Lyons.

Why did Rita and her sister and brother choose Australia? It was after all a long way to go and Argentina, where many Friulians had already established a presence, was a lot closer. There were no assisted passages. Rita and her sister, like Albano before them, paid their own fares in cash. A one way ticket, tourist class, cost 48 pounds.

The answer to 'why Australia?' is of course a practical one.

Albano wanted to emigrate. He said he had to go to Australia or Argentina. One friend went to Argentina. He promised to call Albano over. To sponsor him. But he never heard from him. Albano said if he wasn't going to Argentina, he was going to Australia. There were some people already in Melbourne from Tarcento. He paid his own fare and a deposit to come back. You know it was a lot of money. He never had the money to pay everything. Somebody signed to guarantee for him for the return fare. The passport, everything was regular and he caught the boat in Genoa.

Around the time Albano emigrated government policy in Australia was being driven by a 'populate or perish' mentality, although assisted passages (discontinued between 1929 and 1938) were strictly restricted to immigrants of British origin. Henry Gullett, who would later share space on the *Orion* with Albano's sisters, had set the pace for the 1920s immigration programs before resigning as director of the Immigration Bureau in 1922. In a pamphlet titled *Unguarded Australia*, published in 1919, Gullett emotively argued for a large increase in Australia's migration intake in order to defend the continent of the Commonwealth against the avaricious desires of European and Asian countries to the north. His absurd 100 million target for Australia was to be made up of British stock and, in the last resort, 'emigrants of the right kind from the Continent of Europe'.[1] Australia was to be kept 'white', protected and populated by English-speaking Brits. Albano being from northern Italy had a slight advantage. Many southern Italians coming to Australia around this time were indentured labourers. In Queensland a popular journal referred to 'black' and 'white' Italians to make the distinction between southerners and northerners.

By the time of the Great Depression, in spite of a policy determined to make Australia an ethnically British community, non-Brits, or 'aliens' as the department labelled them, were taking a foothold. James Jupp in *Immigration* points out that, in spite of being made to feel unwelcome, by the 1930s 'small communities of Jews, Italians, Greeks, Germans, Chinese, Maltese and Croatians were able to sustain themselves'[2] and were forming unobtrusive but closeknit communities in parts of Melbourne, Sydney and Brisbane. Rita's description of Albano's early years in Melbourne is a familiar story of the immigrant working to beat the odds.

Albano came down from Genoa to Port Melbourne. He stayed in Melbourne for a while, working in restaurants washing dishes or something like that. He never practised any cooking. After a while he went to Adelaide. He worked there with a concrete manufacturer. One day he went to work with the boss. He was in the back of the truck with the machines, not in the front. The machine shifted in the truck and fell on his leg. The machine broke his leg and he was more than six months in hospital. They stuck it up the wrong way and they had to break it again. He had no insurance but maybe his boss helped. He had a lot of problems.

When the Depression came it was very hard to find work but Rita cannot remember her brother being without work for long except for his accident. As late as 1935 money was still being allocated to building the Hawthorn Boulevard as part of a relief project. An unemployed family man received just ten shillings a week. Shunned by the English-speaking locals the small Italian groups helped one another.

When Rita arrived in Australia in 1935 attitudes to immigration were as varied as they are today. Great Britain was reported in *The Age* of 28 September as encouraging its dominions throughout the Empire to increase their migration intake from 'nations with bursting boundaries'. Such a move was thought to be beneficial to the Empire's defence and also a way of boosting the Empire's dominance throughout the world at a time of increasing instability. There was no suggestion in the report that the 'Mother Country' should do the same. At the other end of the spectrum, in Brisbane, Sir Raphael Cilento warned the annual meeting of the New Settlers League on 9 October that immigration was a hazard. According to Cilento, Australia's population was in a precarious position and Australia's 300 000 unemployed faced little prospect of finding jobs with competition from an inflow of new settlers.

In the 1930s Australia's immigration policy hardened against non-British immigrants by actively discouraging them. In Queensland, where Anglophile attitudes were more prevalent, immigrants of Nordic and German origin were tolerated. The British Royal Family was of German descent, after all.

In spite of Sir Raphael's dire warnings and the immigration bars of the time, Rita and Elisa joined Albano in Melbourne. They were part of a growing swell of non-British immigrants who were establishing a family reunion program well in advance of official programs four decades later. The immigration policy of encouraging sponsorship or nominations from settlers already in Australia meant that as one group, usually the males, settled into life Down Under they would quickly sponsor family members or *paesani* to join them. In the five years before 1940 nearly 40 000 non-British Europeans migrated to Australia, 10 000 of them Italian. They would swell the numbers of 'aliens' considerably on the eve of the great holocaust to come. When Rita arrived in Australia Italian-born settlers made up just under half of one per cent of the population. Today around 40 per cent of Australian Italians live in Victoria.

Behind them they left everything. Most did not understand the chasm created by 12 000 miles. Rita thought she was coming for a year or two but it was 39 years before she went back to Italy. She and her sister never again saw their mother or any of their three siblings who remained in Italy. In 1949 Albano went back for his first visit. Unknown to him as the ship left Australia his mother's funeral was being held in Tarcento the same day.

By the time Rita and Elisa joined Albano, he had been running his own business for a couple of years in partnership with Giuseppe, another Friulian. It was a remarkable transformation of circumstances in a few years. It was driven by a natural instinct in spite of the hard times.

Albano was back in Melbourne. He had worked for different wine shops and fruit shops and in various jobs. Then he went into partnership. The partner became my husband. They were in a fruit shop in Sydney Road, Brunswick. It used to be a hat shop and the owner of the shop offered it to them. She had done nothing much for years. She said if you want to buy the shop you have to pay me such and such. So they started a partnership. Albano did very well in the fruit business. After a year or so they sold the shop and opened another in High Street, Northcote.

For many decades one of the great features of Australian life has been the Italian family fruit shop. In Melbourne every suburb seems to have one and in many shopping locations they are more numerous than pubs. Whatever the season, fruit and vegetable shops in Australian cities offer the shopper an amazing array of fresh produce. The family greengrocer has even managed to survive the big competitor supermarket and its Hollywood-style merchandising.

The Italian fruiterer in Australia developed out of the rural success of Italian farmers in the south-west and south-east corners of the continent. Like the Germans of South Australia in the wine industry, Italian farmers were able to produce valuable foodstuffs from intense cultivation so unlike the vast expansive cattle, sheep and wheat farms of British settlers. In the towns and cities other Italians marketed the produce through to the Australian consumer.

Jock Collins in his chapter in *Australia's Italians* explains how by the 1940s about one half of Australia's Italians were already employed in small 'catering' businesses—espresso bars, restaurants, wine shops, fruit and vegetable markets. The reasons for this were expedient. Only a small amount of capital was needed to start, they were less subject to union interference, the businesses lent themselves readily to the use of family labour, they could be maintained with a minimum of English and the work premises provided ideal and cheap housing for the immigrant family.

Having a business meant having a home on the premises. Shop owners were neighbours and family life centred on the shop. In Albano's shop, work began early in the morning and on some nights finished when the shop closed at midnight. Shopping hours permitted late night trading. Under the *Factories and Shops Act 1915* fruit and vegetable shops were classified as 'Fourth Schedule' shops. This meant there were no limits to trading hours except between the months of May and September. Most stayed open whenever there was the chance of trade. Between May and September, regulation closing time varied from 7 pm mid-week to 9 pm on Fridays and 10 pm on Saturdays. Rita's weekly salary was two pounds. At the time machinists and temporary women employees in the public sector earned nearly double that. The basic wage was three pounds nine shillings.

When Rita arrived in Australia she went to work in her brother's fruit and vegetable shop. Two years later, after marrying her brother's original partner, she moved from living over her brother's fruit shop to living over her husband's fruit shop in Smith Street, Collingwood. The fruit business was to be her business for the next 28 years. The weekend Rita married she finished work in her brother's shop at midnight on Saturday, had Sunday off while the wedding took place and started work in her husband's shop that week. She doesn't remember any holiday in between. Anna and I laugh at such absurdity but Rita shrugs and grins as if to say, 'What else could we do?'.

When Albano's two sisters agreed to join him in Melbourne they unwittingly displaced his partner, Giuseppe. He also had come from Friuli, but from a town called Percoto which is so small it can't be found on most maps. It is south of Udine close to Pavia di Udine. Having grown up just a few miles from Rita it was only when Giuseppe was thousands of miles away from their home towns that he met her. Even so he wasn't keen. Giuseppe had gone into business with Albano a year or so before the sisters arrived in Australia. On hearing that Albano had sent for 'the girls', Giuseppe made it clear he would not continue in the partnership if women were to join them. So he left the Northcote shop and started out alone in Smith Street. Two years later everything was different. Rita and Giuseppe were married.

Italian weddings can be very big affairs. It is not uncommon for families to hire a town hall. But Rita's wedding was quite different and there was nothing common about it. St Patrick's Cathedral is a couple of blocks from the top end of exclusive Collins Street and the Melbourne Club. Here the Catholic Church blessed the union of Rita and Giuseppe. Then the happy couple took twenty-five people to dinner at the Latin, a Melbourne city restaurant where even Sydney restaurant critic Leo Schofield would have been satisfied. In the wedding group photo Anna takes down from a shelf Rita, looking very like her daughter Isabella, is dark and beautiful in a black velvet coat with a shoulder wide fur collar. Her dress is a full length ivory crepe. The outfit has been tailored to Rita's design by another dressmaker as it is bad luck for a bride to make her own wedding dress. There is no hint in the photo of the long working hours that paid the bill at the Latin. It was 14 November 1937.

For their time, Rita and Giuseppe were unusual in many ways among Australia's Italian community. Many of the immigrant Italian settlers were single men. Most did not find Italian girls to marry in Australia. This meant either intermarriage with non-Italians or staying single. In Albano's case he did not marry until he was fifty and to find a bride he went back to Italy.

Down the hill below Rita's house the fringes of Kew give

way to the Yarra River, Melbourne's great divide, which snakes its way for miles between Ivanhoe and South Yarra separating those who have made their pile from those who have not. In walking distance from Rita's front door are a few remaining mansions built in the heyday of Melbourne's colonial Protestant ascendancy. But fortunes come and go or are passed on to newer groups. Rags-to-riches Collingwood-born Catholic John Wren owned one of these mansions for a while. Raheen, former home of Melbourne's Catholic Arch-bishops and now showpiece of business couple Richard and Jeanne Pratt, is another. Today many are no longer family homes. They have become the workplaces of institutions. Burke Hall, Campion Hall and John Wren's old mansion (setting for Australian author Frank Hardy's *Power Without Glory* which included a fictional scandal about Mrs Wren) are now owned by the Jesuits.

A block up the hill from Rita's house and passing each of these yesteryear landmarks is Studley Park Road. Going west towards the city, it winds down into the flat of Abbotsford and Collingwood as it crosses the Yarra. There it changes to prosaic Johnston Street before continuing on its route inter-secting the commercial and industrial inner suburbs for a few kilometres and passing Hoddle Street then Smith Street along the way.

For part of Collingwood's Smith Street, from Johnston Street to Victoria Street, there is a kilometre of shops. Just minutes from Melbourne's central business district, in 1937 this bustling commercial strip bordered low life Gertrude Street at one end and the chocolate empire of MacRobertsons' factories at the other. It boasted small and large stores of every variety. There was Treadways, and Allans Photographic Studios, ham and beef shops with fresh rabbits for ten pence a pair, cake stores where one penny worth of fruit cake could be cut into three slices and a bag of broken biscuits cost the same. The shops were dominated by the grand old lady of department stores, Foy & Gibson, boasting its own 'two miles of mills' from Fitzroy to the back streets of Collingwood, producing merchandise from furniture to hats. In Collingwood's industrial maze beyond the shopping walk-ways there were trades making fabrics, yarns, buttons, knitted garments, clothing and footwear and heavy engineering such as the products of the vast British United Shoe Machinery Company. For decades Smith Street and the streets around it were evidence of (protected) manufacturing Victoria at its best. In the thick of it newcomers like Rita and her family made a fresh start with old skills.

Driving along major through roads as one nears the city centre, whether in Melbourne or Sydney, late nineteenth century two storey shop architecture lines the streets. For nearly a century wide verandahs of corrugated iron came out across the footpaths to hug the kerbs and shelter shoppers from the heat and rain, until the 1960s when age and modernity began bringing many down and renovating others. The shops are designed like Victorian terraced houses. At the front a large room with floor length window on to the street forms the shop. Behind and above are rooms to live in. Smith Street, Collingwood was one of those verandah-lined thoroughfares. Rita and Giuseppe operated their fruit shop there, near Johnston Street, for nine years.

Smith Street was a very big house. The bedrooms were upstairs. The ceilings were not low like these modern houses. It was a big fruit shop a couple of blocks from Johnston Street. MacRobertsons were the owners. Very tiring. Up and down the stairs. If someone had measles or chicken pox or something it was up and down all the time. I was very sick in the back.

The high ceilings meant there were more stairs to climb while Rita moved between her babies sleeping upstairs and the shop below. On occasions there was help from young girls paid to look after the children for busy periods such as Saturday morning. However, when one of the babysitters took to throwing the baby's milk down the sink rather than coax the baby to drink it, Rita thought twice about home help. But she did have a man to help serve in the shop. Rita's management philosophy was simple and as a management rule it is probably the key to higher productivity. *If you work for yourself it is like three people doing the work. It's the same in any business. You should work for yourself. You know what you are doing. You have to pay more to someone else and you are never sure they are doing what you want.*

Rita did not need a course in business management at a

taxpayer-funded university to be successful in management. A commonsense approach underpinned the family business and it has been central to tens of thousands of other small Australian businesses. It was an instinctive survival strategy against industry regulations and the cost of employing staff. Under the *Factories and Shops Act 1936* Wages Boards had the power where appropriate to 'determine any industrial matter whatsoever in relation to any trade or branch of trade' and to determine all matters relating to (among other things) days and hours of work, pay and wages, rights and duties of employers and employees, terms and conditions of employment and 'non-employment', employee/employer relations, employment matters related to sex and age, demarcation of functions of employees and employers, and all questions of what is fair and right in any industrial matter. In this climate of industrial regulation, and where migrant employers sought a living with imperfect language skills, small businesses could not maintain a strict adherence to the industrial catechism and expect to make profits. Employing family members was one way around the regulatory overlay. One of Rita's friends gave up his shop when his daughter left home to get married. *He sold the business because his daughter got married. She wasn't going to work with him any more. He just stayed at home then. He had developed a lot of properties over the years and he used to go around collecting the rents.* One of the rents he collected was paid by Rita and Giuseppe when they took over the fruit shop he gave up.

Working six days a week, staying open late, keeping employee costs to a minimum and living frugally might feed and shelter the family but it brought no easy pot of gold. It was not until 1949 that the family bought a motor vehicle even though transport was essential to their business. To fetch the fruit and vegetables from the market each day Rita's husband used a horse and cart. In twentieth century Collingwood the horse was stabled in Otter Street near St Joseph's church. Years later at their second shop in Abbotsford there was a stable in the yard behind and when the car replaced the horse the stable became the garage.

We are well into the story now and Rita is reflective. Sometimes when she speaks she uses a bit of Italian among the English. A favourite one is her 'per' instead of 'for'. I enjoy hearing it because it's part of Rita's character. Although a foreign language illiterate I can understand what it means and I like the way it softens the English. If Anna explains occasionally in Italian some of the finer points of the discussion I am simply delighted to have the help of an expert. But Rita is conscious of her English. And suddenly she elaborates on how it feels, without any prompting, in the middle of answering another question.

It wasn't easy for her to learn English although working in the shop helped a little. Albano had wanted her to attend classes when she first arrived in Australia but they had no idea where to go. There was no help given in those days. Then Albano decided that their sister Elisa, who was the older and therefore not so easy to order about in the shop, could look for work. Elisa found a position in Georges department store making model outfits for Georges' own label. But Rita was told she must work in the shop. Rita could be an independent businesswoman in her home town but in Australia she was in the care of her brother who acted like a father. She explains all this in a few words.

After I worked a little bit in the shop, managing with 'yes please' and 'thank you', my brother said you've got to stay here. Because my sister had a job at Georges. Albano forced me to work in the fruit shop. He said my English would be alright. He would teach me. But then I start there and I finish there; my life goes by in the fruit shop.

To Rita the challenge was more than knowledge of a language. It was confidence in using it. Her nephew who was educated at university in Italy had perfect English and yet was intimidated by having to speak it in public—unlike Rita who would always try to manage.

Staying in the business my English got a little better. Even with the babies I liked to stay in the business. Once you are out of the business you don't talk to anybody in English. After my marriage I could go by myself to town. I caught the tram in Smith Street. I knew where to go. My nephew Renato, he was very slow. He was frightened to go by himself; he didn't like to go and ask people which train to catch. He was frightened about his English.

Language is clearly something Rita can feel strongly about. Standing at the deli counter of my local Woolworths store and helping a well spoken Chinese lady pronounce 'cabanossi' I think of Rita. I remember her again at the fish market in David Jones' food department when the elegantly dressed middle aged lady next to me points at the glass and, with a thick European accent, asks in limited English for 'that one please'.

For a moment in the interview Rita digresses to argue that all emigrants should learn the language of the host country before leaving home. But, as we point out, this would have kept her in Italy. Moreover, of all the family, Renato was the only one who then spoke English and also the only one who could not settle successfully in Australia. She finds she is caught between. There is no easy solution. But on one point she is adamant. There should be easily available classes for immigrants when they arrive. And newcomers who don't speak English should be made to learn it.

When Rita, her husband Giuseppe, brother Albano and sister Elisa came to Australia nobody helped them learn the language. They picked it up on the job. At home naturally they spoke Italian or Friulano just as Australians would talk in English when staying in Italy. Messages on the radio meant little and for a while they did not have a radio. When Giuseppe bought a wireless after his first child was born his friends looked at it speechless.

If Rita feels she has suffered by not being adept at English her children certainly gained by growing up bilingual. Anna, Mirella and Isabella read and speak Italian as if they had grown up in Friuli. Rita speaks to them constantly in Italian or Friulano. Her second daughter, Mirella, is especially proficient in reading the unique Friulano language. Rita's home is like a language workshop. Foreign language students in Australia would envy her children's linguistic advantages. And Rita has always encouraged them. *To the girls I speak Italian [Friulano] all the time. It is nice to know the mother language too. Maybe Anna now doesn't practise it much but if she has to use the language she can.*

When I first met Anna, at the Mercy College in Fitzroy (the Academy), we were beginning Year 12. A last minute change in my education had sent me into a new school for my final year where I was quickly adopted by a group of Italian girls after befriending one of them on the tram home from school. Franca, Lena, Angela, Ombretta and Anna took me in. Being a friend of one meant you were a friend of all. In Robert Pascoe's *Buongiorno Australia: Our Italian Heritage* there is a photo of the Year 11 Italian class at the Academy in 1986. The pretty Latin faces in the picture are uncanny in their likeness to those of the group I knew in 1965. In those twenty years their features became familiar in everyday Australia. At Melbourne University where most of my school group ended up we would meet between lectures in the library or the Union. I joined the Italian Club without ever studying Italian. It was renowned for its parties. Later on we caught up at weddings and for a time kept in touch. Today I ask after the others when I see Anna.

All of my Italian school friends studied Italian at regular Saturday morning classes at University High School—the Saturday School of Modern Languages. For years 'Italian school' had meant Saturday school. At the Academy they would compare notes and help each other over difficult exercises. While they intrigued me helping one another with their translations of Dante, I would attempt superiority in the rarer features of pure mathematics. As it turned out their Italian far outdid my pure maths and most of them went on to establish solid careers as language teachers. At Monash University where Anna was not able to take Italian she transferred to Spanish with ease. In recent years she and her older sister Isabella have developed Alta Vita, renovating Australian homes around fine imported Italian homewares and Schiffini-designed kitchens—the first in Australia. Their familiarity with northern Italy and the Italian language has been important in their success.

But cultural gain for the children of immigrant parents comes at a cost. 'Foreign' can also mean outsider. In new worlds like Australia each new immigrant group will eventually face the ignorance and prejudice of 'locals', descendants of earlier immigrant groups. With the outbreak of World War II Rita and her family were not only foreign, they were officially suspect.

In June 1940, after remaining officially neutral for the first months of the war, Italy became Germany's ally. Half a world away Italians like Rita's family, who had chosen to leave Mussolini's Italy, were told by the Australian Government that they must report to the police station every week. Under the National Security (Aliens Control) Regulations, membership however distant of any political group regarded as hostile to the Allied cause could make an enemy alien liable to internment. Even refugees from Germany and countries occupied by the Germans needed to prove that they did not have associations that made them a risk to the war effort. Under the guidelines for the Aliens Control legislation this meant for example that German people of Jewish background who had fled Germany because of the Nazis were classified as 'enemy aliens', and needed to prove that their loyalty to Australia was such that they could not be prevailed upon by the enemy. Many like the group of Jewish refugees who arrived in Australia on board the *Dunera* were interned nonetheless. Paranoid and jingoistic attitudes ruled the day.

Newspaper reports occasionally illustrated the nature of feelings towards outsiders at the time. On 8 January 1940 a bushfire in Gippsland was reported in *The Age* as follows:

> Bairnsdale, Sunday. Damage estimated at nearly £2000 was caused by a fire which swept grazing properties and crown lands in the Nurngurner district on the Gippsland Lakes on Friday. R. Travers lost 500 acres of grass and practically the whole of the fencing. Thomas Helir lost fencing, two stacks of hay and ten acres of grass. Italian settlers also suffered losses.

For the Chinese community, whose numbers in Australia were vigorously opposed under the White Australia Policy, there were brownie points however. Chinese market gardeners began delivering a daily supply of fresh vegetables to the Australian troops in training. Under the heading 'Our Chinese' *The Age* on 27 January 1940 patronisingly presented the following mention for good behaviour: 'Chinese are almost always good citizens and generous in a worthy cause. Soldiers of the 2nd AIF in camp at the showgrounds have had a practical demonstration of the good will of a section of the people who thoroughly appreciate their treatment as subjects protected by the British flag'. China was clearly an ally.

Enforcement of the Aliens Control regulations varied

according to circumstance. Rita and Giuseppe were known to the local constables who regarded them as friends.

The police in the street passed every day. Sometimes they would say it didn't matter to report. They knew we were alright. They went up and down all the time. They knew all the people. Sometimes my husband went down to the police station. And the police sometimes came into the shop—to have a glass of beer.

Not everyone was like that, however. One neighbour a couple of doors away, a retired nurse who lived above the bootmaker's, stopped coming to Rita's shop after the outbreak of war. She stopped talking to the family, refusing even to say hello. A day or two after war was declared one passer-by stood outside the shop yelling, 'Don't go in there. Dagos. Dagos'. While there were many who ignored the official line and were friendly, anti-Italian feeling was evident. At times the police would come and move the troublemakers on. It was unpleasant but tolerable. By the first year of the war Rita was expecting her second child. As her labour time drew near in November the shop and the stairs became an added burden. One night, with her hospital bag packed and ready, a climb of the stairs brought sharp pains and the signs that a birth was imminent.

I lay down on the bed for a few minutes to rest after the steps and the baby started coming very quickly. My husband asked if he should call Mrs Hastings. That was the old woman who was the retired nurse who wouldn't speak to us. She came in but she touched nothing. She was waiting for the doctor. But my husband had to stop a car outside to take him down to Clifton Hill to fetch the doctor. The doctor came in his pyjamas. He had a car.

When the doctor arrived young Mirella was born without mishap. It fell to the neighbour, who had so distrusted her Italian fruiterers, to clean up. And she did. Rita remembers feeling sorry for her.

From then on relations were restored and the neighbour was very friendly bringing little presents for the children. Whether convinced by the doctor that Italians were human too or simply overcome by the experience, it is not clear why she melted. But it is consistent with a recurring phenomenon to be found in Australia. Racial tension is rarely ideologically based and human contact with neighbours, workmates and other social experience often wears away prejudice. At an official level things were different. Under the Alien Control regulations aliens were prevented from possessing or using, except with a special permit, all manner of firearms and ammunition (of course) as well as, among other things, carrier pigeons, motor vehicles, telephones, wireless apparatus or cameras. For Giuseppe and Rita there was no problem about a car or phone which they did not own, but Giuseppe was told to put away his humble wireless for the duration of the war. In November 1940 at the congress of the returned soldiers (RSL) a resolution was passed urging the government to intern all enemy aliens regardless of background or circumstance. The particular fear was expressed that Italian fishermen on the New South Wales and Victorian coastline could provide valuable information to the enemy at sea. Giuseppe wasn't a fisherman but he was Italian and he did have a wireless. It could all look the same to some.

Australia's internment of wartime aliens, enhanced by its unequivocal jargon, was a rude and raw policy thrown up by the hysteria of world conflict and a slavish following of British example. In its implementation, however, the program was eventually diluted after public protest and distaste at indiscriminate internment and its implications. In addition the application of the security powers moderated somewhat after November 1940 when aliens were able to submit objections to an Alien Tribunal. Throughout the period of the internment program it was the Italian community which seems to have suffered most. While at any stage only a small percentage of either community was interned, the number of Italians interned was three times greater than the number of Germans.

Newspaper reports confirmed this imbalance from time to time. During 1942 local prejudice against 'aliens' became noticeably vocal. But Italian settlers were the only ethnic group continually singled out in the press reports. This is surprising when one considers how relatively small a part the Fascist Government of Italy played in the war effort.

In March 1942 a district council meeting at Bacchus Marsh,

west of Melbourne, protested that 'aliens' were well on the way to controlling fruit and vegetable markets in the Shire of Mulgrave. The meeting accused 'avaricious' foreigners, who were presumably supporting the enemy, of forcing out gallant and patriotic Australians who were contributing to the war effort. The circular from the meeting advised that '. . . Italians had crowded together like rabbits in burrows' and it was time 'that state of affairs was cleaned up'. In April of the same year, at a meeting of the Colac district council, concern was angrily expressed that 'aliens' were buying up the good onion land at 'ridiculous' prices of ten and twenty pounds an acre. Italians (again) were getting control (this time) of the onion business. Apparently this was due to having shifted these alien groups away from the coastal Otways 'because of the danger of having them close to the sea'. One councillor, G. McCarthy, said he 'would not like to trust Italians to fight for Australia'. A consensus was reached that Italians should be prevented from leasing land or having working shares in it.

Settlers like Rita and Giuseppe were damned if they did and damned if they did not. They could not take part in the war effort because they were born in a country at war with Australia, yet if they went on living normally, trying hard not to give offence, they were branded as privileged.

Like the majority of Italians Giuseppe was not interned. But he was conscripted as the government toughened manpower policies following Japan's entry into the war. After February 1942 the Alien Service regulations enabled the government to call up for civil service a pool of alien labour. A letter arrived at the shop soon after, telling Giuseppe he must present himself as an alien conscript—in Wangaratta, over 200 kilometres north of Melbourne. Rita recalls the occasion. *He had to bring everything himself. He had to take his own blankets and a mattress. I bought a mattress, cheap, in Treadways. He went to Wangaratta and chopped wood. In the bush.*

Meanwhile at the end of the street another Italian, who had become an Australian citizen, was spared the trauma that Giuseppe and his family faced.

During the winter of 1942 fuel supplies reached record lows. Forestry districts grumbled about government mismanagement of the delivery of wood to the cities and threatened action against the use of alien labour to split piles of firewood. Against this backdrop Giuseppe found his way to Wangaratta and the camp that formed part of the Alien Construction Corps. His pay was subsistence level. Workers lived makeshift in tents. In spite of the National Security Regulations that threatened onerous fines of a hundred pounds as well as six months imprisonment for any resistance, conditions in the camps were so bad that in Queensland, in early August, a group of Alien construction workers defied the government and went out on strike.

Back in Melbourne Rita, with two children under three, had to manage as best she could to live and cope with their shop which was also their home. Rita was on her own. The only solution was to close the shop. The stock dwindled away by the end of the week. Rita, like other women in small migrant businesses, was an equal partner and vital in the drive, direction and work that had to be done in the family business. But Giuseppe was the link with the market world and the supply of stock. That was the man's role. Without Giuseppe to harness up the horse and transport fresh produce each day Rita could only shut the shop.

But there was still the rent. Then a kinder fate stepped in, illustrating that tolerance and goodwill existed also, not just prejudice and racial bigotry, in Australian society.

I finished off the stock, sold it. And shut the shop.
MacRobertsons were the owners. An agent came every
week. The rent was three pounds. MacRobertsons found
out the shop was shut and they sent a man down. He
told me not to pay until the shop opened again.
Somebody had told them what happened to my husband.
They said there is no income so you don't have to pay us.

And MacRobertsons won Rita's respect forever.

It could have been a lot worse and Rita does not say much about how it felt. She was very isolated with two small babies but even more so because her English was still not very well developed. Who to talk to? It was lonely. During the years of internment and alien conscription the government took little interest in the wives or children, interning mostly only the men. To be left alone with children, no income and little

English was in some cases just as harsh an ordeal as life in an alien camp. There was no knowing for Rita how long she would have to manage like this.

Giuseppe's stay in the conscription camp was cut short by an accident. He injured his shoulder and was sent back to Melbourne for treatment in St Vincent's Hospital. After that he was allowed to return to his family. The shop had been shut for six months. At about this time the Victorian (Country Party) Premier Mr Albert Dunstan spoke publicly about his regret that small Australian shopkeepers had lost their businesses due to wartime duties. His regret was that alien businesses were capitalising on the misfortune of true Australians. Rita and Giuseppe might have wondered at his remarks.

The war ended and in 1946 Rita and Giuseppe became Australian citizens. They moved shop to Johnston Street, Abbotsford, just across the road from what had been John Wren's illegal betting shop. All forms of off-course betting were still illegal. In Johnston Street the horse had a stable in the backyard, there were no stairs to climb and it was a good business. Rita and Giuseppe were still paying rent. It was years before they could afford to buy the freehold.

For fourteen years Rita worked with Giuseppe in the shop at Abbotsford, a picture of what James Jupp in *Immigration* refers to as the greengrocer stereotype of Australia's prewar Italian. In the 1950s and 1960s migrants from Italy like Rita and Giuseppe were overtaken by a new wave of predominantly southern Italians. These later arrivals were more likely to take jobs as industrial and construction workers. However their inner suburban settlement in suburbs like Leichhardt in Sydney or Carlton and Brunswick in Melbourne was a transition phase and their children rapidly moved into the middle classes through education or business success. Most bought their own homes within a decade or so.

In the 1950s Rita and Giuseppe were the image of small business success with a business they owned, no debts, a car, a family of five and all Australian citizens. Prime Minister Bob Menzies, with his sentimental appeal to the middle classes as the 'forgotten people', could be proud of them (if he had ever thought of them at all). Yet success in business meant long hours serving in the shop for all the family. In the 1950s while Rita ran the fruit shop the average 'mother' in Australian suburbia spent 45 hours of her week in the kitchen. While Rita and Giuseppe continued to live behind the shop the Australian dream, achieved by other Australians, was a home of one's own on a quarter acre block. Then Giuseppe died in 1960. Except for his allowance in the wartime Construction Corps and some hospitalisation as a result of that experience he had taken nothing in the way of handouts from his new country. Nor had he ever asked for any.

Anna's pasta is a temptation by now. We continue the interview over lunch, tape recorder off and talking intensely as we always do. To finish off we have soft cheese and olives with Italian coffee, a meal now so familiar to Australians thanks to thousands of Italian immigrants. Rita and Anna have another engagement and I have another interview, this time in a Carmelite convent. But we keep talking and I ring the convent to say I am running late.

There are no regrets for Rita. Her life has been a happy one. She is uncomplicated, practical and generous. Having demonstrated her natural talent as a tailor dressmaker and built a business from it before she was thirty, Rita did not use those skills to earn her living once in Australia. Instead she tailored for her family. Designer style clothes came from her sewing trunk until she 'retired'.

I do only tailoring for the family. If you are working in the shop, cooking and everything, you don't have the time. Now I don't want to do any. After the first communion of Margherita, the last baby of Mirella, I did nothing after. The dress for the first communion, I made it and said this is the last. Finished. I can't see.

Rita tailored for 67 years although she was paid for her skill for only thirteen years. Studies show that the skills of many immigrants like Rita are even today underutilised when they come to Australia. But Rita's business acumen does live on with Isabella and Anna in their shop, while Mirella, a pharmacist, has managed many businesses throughout her career.

In 1974 Rita went back to Europe for the first time after migrating to Australia. All her immediate family had died. But she met Giuseppe's family for the first time. They had lost their brother before he could make a trip back to see them. Rita came instead. Elisa, Rita's sister, had never made it back. She died in 1973 before there was a chance to go home for a visit. And by then, as for Rita, mother and siblings were dead.

Going back for some of Rita's migrant friends in Australia was an early priority even when travelling took up so much time and it meant leaving businesses for months. When Rita was about to leave Italy in 1935 one friend was already back for a visit. Giuseppe however believed he should invest in his children's education first and think about a trip home only when that was achieved. He also believed that a lot of property was not as important as a good education.

As immigrant Friulians, Rita and Giuseppe will be numbered with the minority. A large number of those who came to Australia from northern Italy have returned home. Southern Italians have been less likely to re-emigrate. The Udinese went back in great numbers before World War II. By 1968 the number of those returning to the Friuli district outnumbered those emigrating from it.

In Australia, three years after Giuseppe's death Rita and her daughters settled for changes of address Australian style and with each move came a more middle class ambience. It took two moves to bring Rita to her present home in Kew. In 1963 the family gave up running the shop in Abbotsford and moved to North Kew into a suburban bungalow modelled on English architecture with a suburban English–Australian garden. Isabella and Mirella worked to keep the family while Anna finished her schooling and university. They kept the shop in Abbotsford and leased it out for years before finally selling it. By 1970 the family had saved enough to build the sort of home they liked, one that satisfied their taste for the cool uncluttered concepts of modern European design. Looking down towards the Yarra at the end of the street and seeing in the distance the industrial suburbs on the other side, where Rita spent her first thirty years in Australia, many would say that Rita has joined those who have 'made their pile'.

Without a doubt Rita and Giuseppe were able to give their family a future that Friuli did not promise in the 1930s. Still, the cousins in Italy have done well too. The peasant population in Italy more than halved between 1951 and 1971. Travelling in Italy is no longer cheap for Australians, and the family in Friuli seems quite affluent now, even alongside their immigrant Australian relatives.

For Rita's children who have affinities with both Europe and Australia, naturally acquired in the course of their upbringing, a dual identity can be a dilemma. For a while Isabella contemplated relocating to Italy after a year spent working there in the early 1970s. Rita was shocked to hear of Isabella's plans and argued strongly that Australia was the better country. Says Anna, 'Now and then the idea rises to the fore again and is gently laid to rest until the next time'.

Recessionary times are a reminder to Rita's family of the transformation in values they have witnessed during their life in Australia. Anna is reminded of her father's plight during the depression of the 1930s when he travelled the countryside as an unemployed immigrant with a suitcase. The family joke was that he spent so long tramping the roads looking for work that even the suitcase handle was broke. When Rita and her daughters see art gallery exhibitions, packed mid-week during a recent recession, there are few comparisons with the hard times they have known.

There is a second generation of Australians now in Rita's family. They are being educated at schools run by the Australian Jesuits and the Loreto nuns. They also speak Italian. Their father is Italian-born, their mother is Rita's daughter Mirella. They know as much (maybe more) about imported Italian clothes and Ferraris as Paul Keating or John Hewson and they join practice and competition matches on Saturdays for tennis and ball games like any other Australian youngster. When they choose to marry their choices will be less influenced by ethnic considerations than were their parents' or grandparents' choices. Yet Italian culture is still a strong element in their lives and it is natural that it will be an important determinant. Figures on the rate of in-marriage among Australian Italians show there have been dips and highs in different periods for various reasons such as the availablity of partners. However, in contrast to immigrant groups generally which have registered high rates of in-marriage, the Italian–Australian in-marriage rate in recent decades has been much lower.

When the 1992 result of *The Australian*/Vogel $15 000 Literary Award was announced the winner turned out to be a Greek woman named Fontini Epanomitis. Her prize-winning book, *The Mule's Foal,* is based on a collection of tales from Greece which she learned from her father and also on the experience of one year in Greece as a twelve year old when she stayed with her grandmother. In an interview shortly after winning the award Fontini Epanomitis explained that neither of her parents had read the manuscript because neither of them reads English. But they know what it is about. Ms Epanomitis joins a list of winners that includes Australian writers like Tim Winton, Kate Grenville, Brian Castro and Tom Flood. Her father thinks the prize is his since he claims to have contributed the best stories in the work.

What Fontini Epanomitis, Rita's family and many other immigrant Australians like them demonstrate is obvious. They are successful. Rita, Elisa, Albano and Giuseppe had no English when they came to Australia yet they became self-employed very quickly and established prosperous family lines. Looking back on the adventure Rita sums it up with a minimum of fuss: 'The business went very well and the partnership was good'.

Lily

CHOOSING the date for her wedding Lily was careful about the number. She finally settled on 6 June because six was lucky. When said in Cantonese it sounds like 'green' and that means a prosperous new start. It was also the Year of the Goat, an animal respected for its straightforwardness and honesty. For Lily the signs were good.

On the Saturday of Lily's wedding we wound our way up from Sydney's Circular Quay and around the Museum of Contemporary Art to the Park Hyatt Hotel at the edge of the Rocks. It was sunny although breezy about the hairline, a spectacular Sydney winter afternoon. Hedonists were everywhere: on water, in shops and galleries, on green stretches and footpaths. You only had to think up a few crocodiles in the harbour to imagine it was Disneyland.

The wedding was a select gathering, just a handful of

friends and family; about forty in all. The ceremony took place in the hotel's 'Library' room where a tall female marriage celebrant, imposing in bouffant French knot and blue-green acetate, took the intended couple through the words they had chosen for their vows, joining them as husband and wife 'according to the laws of Australia'. Maurice, from Lebanon, promised to love and honour Lily, from Canton, and at least five flashing cameras witnessed the event.

At Maurice and Lily's wedding the guest list spoke volumes about an accelerating flux in the Australian identity. The five or six tables toasting the health of the newly wedded couple consisted of Chinese, Lebanese, Italians, Greeks and Anglo-Celts. Some were relatives, some were friends. Among the small number of children present was Lily's three year old granddaughter, with her honey oval face and black hair. Her father is Italian and her mother Chinese. The menu offered very Australian eye fillets of steak and our tables of eight or ten filled a room furnished and panelled with Australian red cedar and matching wallpaper in the style of a regency stripe. Outside, in the main dining area of the hotel, Japanese and American tourists blended with well off locals distinguished only by their accents.

Lily met Maurice when she was forty. Maurice was a lot younger. She was working as a beautician in the Myer department store at Burwood in Sydney and had a mixed bunch of work friends—one English, one Italian, one Greek, one 'Australian'. Maurice met three of them—Lily, Joanne and Edna—at the Canterbury Leagues Club and took a fancy to Lily. But she needed a lot of convincing. She had very little experience of dating. And she could tell that Maurice thought her flawless pretty face told him she was only twenty-five. She was also a little wary about Lebanese men. So her friends from Myer gave Maurice a quick ultimatum: 'Look after Lily or you will have all of us to deal with. Lily has been through a lot'. Maurice, of course, was a perfect gentleman and patiently courted Lily, with eventual success.

Lily and Maurice have been my friends since 1984 when architect/builder Harold Johnston, recommended by mutual friend and writer Chris Koch, brought an army of mixed ethnic tradesmen to transform our Sydney real estate pur-

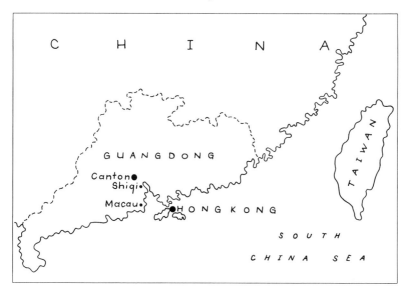

chase after a move from Melbourne. Four functioning flats were converted into one overly large turn-of-the-century house in a record time of five days. Maurice emerged as star performer, rewiring 60 squares of up-and-down in three days and staying on to mop up after others had left tasks unfinished as they sped home for the Christmas break. Maurice was the first electrician I have known who turned up for work in a Mercedes. It was not long before we met Lily.

In 1991 I first heard Lily talk happily about her life in China and subsequent move to Australia. We were catching up with news over yum cha in a Chinese restaurant in Strathfield, not far from where a gunman would go berserk some months later in the shopping plaza. Yum cha with Lily and Maurice is a favourite lunching mode. Lily summons dishes in Cantonese from scurrying waiters and to see what is on the 'menu' examines little hot bamboo tureens as they are wheeled past. While the queue outside waited patiently for a seat inside we lunched in our privileged space that had been acquired when Lily arranged something with the proprietor. She is a good customer.

That day Lily spoke about her recent trips back to Canton, first with Maurice, then with her daughter Sandie and granddaughter Tenille. She was clearly excited about the new freedoms, impressed with the creeping westernisation of her old home district and just as excited that she could go home to see what remnants of the past remained. We looked through the holiday snapshots, one in particular of a substantial two storey home in pre-Mao architecture with elaborate European influences. It was Lily's family home, abandoned for decades under the rule of the Communists and now inhabited by an old uncle who had returned from Hawaii to spend his last years there. Forty years on, China has become a holiday place for Lily on infrequent overseas trips. It is a sort of reverse escape.

A year after our yum cha in Strathfield and a few weeks after her wedding I called for lunch one Saturday at Lily's town house in Sydney's Bankstown. With me were two tape recorders and a supply of blank tapes. Lily will never write her story down. Her formal schooling lasted only a few years.

Lily was born late in 1936 in Shiqi in the district of Zhongshan not far from where Dr Sun Yat Sen was born. There were no birth certificates to register the date. Her village is now in the heartland of the Chinese economic miracle of the 1990s with annual growth rates of 15 and 20 per cent. Buses pour in daily from the border with Macau, depositing their tourist loads at shabby new hotel restaurants to sample local cuisine accompanied by drinks of Coca-Cola in middy-sized outmoded glass bottles. Then it is on, weaving the dusty roads between bicycles, carts and the occasional Mercedes all with drivers that show minimum interest in road codes or two way traffic. The tourists look out over duck ponds and vegetable fields in patchwork order right up to the edges of candy-coloured, three storey box-like houses, each proclaiming the arrival of rural capitalism. Trees and electric light poles equally are coated in a layer of red-brown dust thrown up by the busy passing of so much movement. Only at the model commune with its polka dot houses and smelly lanes, complete with a commune shop trading wares below photos of Mao Zedong and Michael Jackson, and at the folk museum and former home of Dr Sun Yat Sen are there vivid reminders of the district's past—some ugly, some grand.

The invasion of China by the Japanese shortly after Lily was born forced Lily's mother to flee with her baby to Macau. At the same time Lily's father was working in his brother's grocery store in Cairns, Australia. Later he spent some of the war years in a fruit shop with a partner in Sydney's Bondi. Meanwhile the infant Lily, mother and grandmother subsisted in an apartment in Macau till lack of money forced them back to China. There they waited for news and money from abroad but the Japanese occupation lasted for years more and no mail came.

For two generations the men of Lily's family pursued the 'Gold Mountain' path in the land of foreign devils. It was a small Australian version of Maxine Hong Kingston's *China Men*, the story of many thousands of Chinese over three generations who risked death for a chance 'to lie stretched out on any part of the Gold Mountain'[1] in America. Lily's Gold Mountain story begins with her grandfather.

My grandpop came out in the 1890s and was a gold digger up in the Atherton Tableland in Queensland. He reckoned those days were really dangerous. People killed you for nothing just to get at the gold you might be about to find. He found some gold and came down to Cairns to get a boat back to China so he could marry my first grandmother. Then he brought her back to Cairns with him.

Mining for a Chinese immigrant to Australia was certainly a dangerous occupation. Resentment against the influx of Chinese on the goldfields of northern Queensland in the last three decades of the nineteenth century resulted in a series of Acts to deny Chinese gold diggers access to new fields. Racial hostility was overt and enshrined in law. Legislation to exclude Chinese was invariably accompanied by violence or threats of violence against Chinese by locals. Vigilante groups were often formed to eject the Chinese from their claims. Cathie May in *Topsawyers: The Chinese in Cairns, 1870–1920* points out that the objections to Chinese on the gold diggings were not just the particular resentment of those directly involved in mining: 'The connection of mining with the nation's finite resources gave it a certain mystique, and even those who encouraged other forms of Chinese enterprise felt that mineral wealth should be reserved for Europeans'.[2]

When grandpop brought his new bride back to Cairns

there was no comfortable berth on board an ocean liner. The trip was a rough introduction to a lonely and ruinously harsh future existence for the first grandmother.

Poor things, they used to take three months to come out on one of those junks. They travelled with no luggage, just what they could wear. Each day they got one mug of water and it was up to each passenger to decide how to use it: either wash with it or drink it. Grandfather said their clothes were full of fleas because they could not wash. And they had to work their way even though they had paid their passage. It was their free choice to come but they were just like prisoners on the boat.

In Cairns there was a small Chinatown area running along Sachs Street between Shields and Spence Streets. Grandpop very quickly left his new wife there and headed back to the camp on the Tableland, although camp life was isolated, dangerous and a hand-to-mouth existence on salted meat and whatever could be scavenged. The first grandmother, who was married at sixteen, managed alone in Cairns housed in small quarters at the back of a joss house.

They lived there and she had Uncle Willie, Uncle Frank, Aunty Jessie and Uncle Robert. She only saw grandpop once in every six months. After the last baby, when she was still only a very young woman in her early twenties, she grabbed up whatever gold grandpop had brought down and she went back to China with a small fortune. She went back to her family because she wanted to buy her own home. But when her baby was about nine months she died of TB. My father was born later because he belonged to a second wife.

Grandpop's second wife married him because he needed a housekeeper. When his first wife left, grandpop spent four years in Cairns before he decided it was time to look in on his children who were being cared for by their grandparents. Once he was home he decided to claim his children but was not able to look after them alone. In China a man could not have a housekeeper that was not married to him. So Lily's grandfather married the woman who had come to help look after his children. She was the daughter of an opium dealer and she had been sold at the age of seven. Marrying Lily's grandfather was a positive step up the social scale. In time she gave birth to Lily's father and a daughter called Gumyee. Eventually she became Lily's 'second grandmother'.

As grandpop grew older and the boys from his first marriage began returning to Cairns he gave up prospecting in Queensland, acquired land in China and lived happily with second grandmother, helped by a flow of money coming back from the next generation in Australia. All Lily's uncles came back to live in Australia and her father followed them. Lily's Aunty Jessie went to America with her Chinese husband when she was eighteen.

In 1901 the newly federated Commonwealth of Australia passed the Immigration Restriction Act to bar the permanent settlement of 'non-white' immigrants. Canada and the United States passed similar legislation to keep out the Asian flow that had built steadily from the time of the first gold rush, and which had gained momentum with news of other sorts of gold to be found in the laundry business, restaurants, food outlets and general retailing emerging from crowded migrant clusters in cities growing with industrial expansion. In Cairns the consequent slowdown in Chinese immigration meant the Chinese 'locals' like Lily's uncles became more familiar to European Australians. These children of earlier Chinese settlers were more Australian than Chinese and were gradually accepted as part of the town culture. Through them, even with the application of colour bars, small numbers of their relatives from China managed to gain temporary entry. Lily's father came and then eventually Lily herself.

Lily is nostalgic when she remembers growing up in China. Before the Communist regime of 1949 successful farmers lived well. Lily's family were rural and landowning. They were neither rich nor poor. In European terms they would be labelled 'kulaks'. Among the older generations of women in Lily's family only her maternal grandmother had had her feet bound. One of Lily's friends laughs when she explains this. 'We were the workers', she says. But women like Lily's grandmother could become efficient in the farming business as Lily's story indicates.

In Macau we had lived in a very small apartment. It was mainly to hide from the Japanese. After a couple of years it was alright to go back to the village. My father could not send any money because of the war so my grandmother, my mother, all of us went to work on the land we had right next to the house. Until 1944 we grew our own rice and if you grew enough rice you could exchange it for other goods. That is how we survived. We also had a lot of lychee trees. We packed the lychees into baskets to sell. Grandmother grew sweet potato and vegetables. Uncle Robert owned the land and grandmother employed some casual help. There was no trouble getting hired help. It was wonderful then in China. It was a beautiful country.

After the war the farming venture prospered further. The uncles all sent back money and the women were able to lease out the farm. *So we had money from everywhere and we were living very well. We even had a maid to clean because it was a big house with a lot of terracotta floors. The land was producing so much rice that the man who leased it was able to give us back a lot of rice each season and still keep his family. We were rich again.*

Lily's idyllic farming life and the ongoing war meant that she did not begin school until she was eleven. Till then she could not read or write. Her mother had been dead for three years when she started school. Then in 1949 the Communists started to take control of Lily's district and everything changed again.

In 1949 the Communists entered our part of the village. They were okay at the beginning, no problem. They did come into the school and changed a lot of what was taught. They wanted people to be more united and everyone equal. There would be no such thing as 'you are richer than I am'. In China there was a lot of rich and poor. The Communists wanted to make the poorer people feel important and to give them more power. It wasn't too bad; we just kept quiet. But then it got hard. We lost everything. They took the house and only gave us one room for my grandmother and me. It was a room with an internal door into a separate room. The Communists took the rest. The soldiers took the house and used the flat farm land to do their training. The poorer people were allowed to farm our land for no rent. Then it became like civil war. You could not even trust your neighbours.

The many accounts that have been written of life in China from 1950 to the 1980s indicate that this early deprivation which Lily and her grandmother suffered was mild in comparison with what followed in the next few decades. Still, it was a great upheaval. Border crossings to Macau were strictly guarded but it was possible to leave China on a temporary pass into Macau if someone gave a guarantee. Their property and livelihood were gone. There was nothing to keep them in China but an unpleasant new regime of bullying soldiers. Lily and her grandmother, who had 'connections', arranged one of these guarantees and left, taking a bus to the border and walking over to the other side. They added their small figures to the growing refugee trickles from mainland China.

As an early refugee from Communist China Lily missed out on the ideological mania that would take a grip on her country for the rest of the century. She missed the Three Antis and Five Antis campaigns and the Anti-Rightist campaigns. She missed the Great Leap Forward when villagers were commanded to 'make steel' by melting down every available cooking pot and utensil in huge furnaces set up in local lots. She missed the famine that followed Mao's edicts which set fantastical economic goals and promptly undermined them with ideologically correct farming instructions destroying China's centuries old rural prosperity. Tens of millions died. Jung Chang, the daughter of two senior Communist Party officials who were both sent to labour camps in the purges, explains the mentality of the horror Lily missed in her book *Wild Swans: Three Daughters of China*: 'This absurd situation reflected not only Mao's ignorance of how an economy worked, but also an almost metaphysical disregard for reality, which might have been interesting in a poet, but in a political leader with absolute power was quite another matter'.[3] And, ultimately, Lily also missed China's period of terror which was euphemistically called the Cultural Revolution.

Lily's grandmother was not so lucky. She returned to her village and was arrested for being rich. She was tied up so tightly that it left a mark on her ankles for the rest of her life. She was a woman in her sixties. In captivity grandmother was made to stand for three days and not allowed to sleep. Then she was released when someone pointed out that the land really belonged to her sons. She was innocent of land-owning. In the mid-1950s she escaped again to Macau and never returned. In 1969 she went to live on Australia's Gold Coast.

Grandmother had gone back to China after Lily was accepted on a student visa into Australia. In Hong Kong Lily had some family connections. Her mother's relations owned a big department store which employed many of the extended family members. However, Lily's mother had died of TB in 1944 and the relationship with that side of the family was distant. Lily's father and uncles were all in Australia. There had been agreements in 1904 and 1912 that Australia would accept officially sponsored students from Japan, India and China. A handful of relatives had come to Australia under these arrangements. In 1950 the Colombo Plan, initiated by Australia's Minister for External Affairs, Percy Spender, ush-ered in a wider program that allowed students from Asia into Australia at the secondary and tertiary level. Lily was a small Chinese girl of fourteen in 1951. But she had no birth certif-icate to prove it. Her schooling had been limited in China to a few years of primary education. If she said she was only eleven her chances of being accepted were enhanced, espe-cially as her nearest relatives were all in Australia and she was virtually an orphan in Hong Kong. So officially, in 1951, Lily became eleven and her Uncle Willie and his wife, who owned the store in Cairns, became her sponsors to bring her to Australia as a student. It was a family reunion but it was also a giant letdown for Lily when she arrived.

What I expected was big buildings like Hong Kong which was all highrise even in those days. Everybody talked about Australia and they said it was a 'Gold Mountain'. They always said, 'Where's your father?' And I replied, 'Oh, my father is gone to the Gold Mountain'. But Cairns was a dusty old place. They didn't have bitumen in all the streets then. When a car went past the dust went up. I was shocked by black people like Aborigines. My aunt had an Aboriginal woman to do the washing and scrub the floors. I was shocked to find out that I had to work

all day in the shop. And my aunt got rid of the
Aboriginal maid and I had to do the washing and
scrubbing as well. I thought I was coming out to go to
school. Instead I became the maid and the shop assistant.
Oh my illusions.

Uncle Willie and his brothers were born in Australia before Federation and thus before the White Australia Policy. Early in the days of the new Commonwealth Government any loopholes in the Immigration Restriction Act had been plugged. By 1905 non-Europeans who had been 'formerly domiciled' in one of the colonies that formed the Commonwealth could no longer gain exemption under the Act. When Lily's uncles arrived back in Cairns there were only exemptions for students and 'merchants', for which they did not qualify, and assistants like 'chefs'. It is no coincidence then that Uncle Willie began work in Cairns as a 'chef' for a Chinese eating house. Later he acquired his own store. He went back to China to marry and later brought Lily's aunt back to Cairns.

From the age of fourteen Lily, who was officially only eleven, worked every day for her uncle and aunt in their general store at 203 Sheridan Street, Cairns. Today in the fast growing tourist town it is the site of a motel. But in 1951 it was the familiar Australian corner store where butter was cut like cheese from the wedge and all manner of purchases could be made, from minor household utensils to basic foodstuffs. This was a primeval time in Australia before supermarkets and icy poles. Uncle Willie's shop was open about fourteen hours a day, seven days a week.

Lily spoke no English and the family communicated in Cantonese. Except for an older daughter the family spoke only rudimentary English for use in business. But Lily's cousin Jessie, having grown up in Cairns and who was 21, spoke English like any Australian. At the time Jessie was one of the few Chinese or Asians employed in a white collar job. She worked in a finance company in Cairns. She became Lily's good friend but mostly she orbited on another plane from her cousin.

To mark her acceptance into the family, Lily's aunt decided her niece would be called Maisie and put that name on Lily's registration papers. Aunty didn't tell her niece what she had done which made Lily look very stupid when she appeared not to know her name as her papers were processed. So Lily began a Cinderella existence as an immigrant in Cairns with no prospect of escape with a shining prince. Her father in Melbourne was too busy with a new wife to care. It was the year Australia's High Court and a referendum poll of 4.7 million Australians denied the Menzies Government the right to ban the Communist Party. It was also only the second year in sixteen years of Menzies Governments and the beginning of a period of relative prosperity for Australians. But it was also to be an era of missed opportunities, especially in adapting to the changing economies of the Asia–Pacific region, which economists and political commentators four decades later would repeatedly point out.

Like Rita in Albano's shop Lily was thrown into an English-speaking society at the deep end.

My cousin was very well educated. My aunty didn't speak good English but Uncle Willie wasn't bad. Actually I learnt from the groceries. The first day in the house my aunty said, 'Now get out there and work'. A lady had come into the shop. She asked me for something. I didn't know what she was asking me but she pointed to it. I learnt 'Apricot Jam'. I have never forgotten it. I knew the ABC because I had some quick lessons in Hong Kong.

Lily's Cinderella story got bleaker. When life in Cairns became more miserable than Lily felt she could endure, she pestered her father in Melbourne to claim her. He had remarried shortly after the end of the war. His new wife was Chinese but she had one English grandmother. She was prone to nervous disorders and did not want her family to know her new husband was previously married. In short she did not want Lily. However, eventually under pressure Lily's father agreed to let her join him in Melbourne. This meant Lily had to travel by train from Cairns only a year after she had begun to learn English. But she was confident and excited at the chance to escape her workhouse.

Even though I didn't speak properly—I couldn't say 'camera', I'd say 'cama'—and I couldn't roll that tongue around, I could understand what was said. I couldn't argue with anyone but I could get by. So I came all the

*way by train with my cousin to Sydney, stopping in
Brisbane first. A friend of my uncle met us in Brisbane
and helped us to change trains. We stayed a week in
Sydney with friends and had a bit of a holiday and then
they put me on the train for Melbourne. My dad and
stepmother met me. I was told I must not call him
'father', just 'uncle'. But everybody said I looked like him
and then they started to ask questions.*

Lily spent only nine months in Melbourne. As the situation
worsened Lily's stepmother threatened to have her sent back
to China. The father intervened, weakly, and managed a
compromise saying that he would help support Lily if she
returned to Cairns.

*My stepmother then bought me a one way ticket to Cairns
and told me I was leaving straight away. I didn't even
have a chance to pack my bag. I left my luggage in
Melbourne and it was never sent on to me. I had five
pounds and a one way ticket. It took three days and I sat
up all the way. In Brisbane I managed to get a taxi to
take me to a friend's house. He helped me get the train to
Cairns. I met a lovely lady on the train who bought me
some food when we stopped in Mackay and I could not
wake up. There was no food on the train and wherever it
stopped you had to get out and buy some. Afterwards this
lady used to write to me at Christmas and Easter. I
couldn't write back but I used to send a card. I think my
cousin Jessie must have written to her once. So then I just
stayed in Cairns.*

Lily's father of course rarely sent any money. At the shop
in spite of the long hours she worked there was no salary,
just food and a few hand-me-down clothes from Jessie. In
time Lily learnt to sew and quickly found she was a natural
tailor. When Jessie asked her to fix up a dress that she could
not finish Lily often got it as a cast off when the style began
to bore her cousin. Occasionally Jessie would take Lily out
and buy her some shoes. But Lily had no money of her own.

*By the end of 1953 things were pretty tough. I was
growing up but I had no money, no clothes, nothing. I
decided I'd look for a job. But I couldn't speak English*

properly and no one wanted to give me a job except for the hamburger shop. The man who owned it, Mr Owen, loved Chinese although he was a real Aussie. I couldn't stand the sight of him but I worked for him on Friday, Saturday and Sunday nights and I got three pounds. I worked all the days, every day, in my aunty's store for nothing. Then my aunty demanded board and I had to pay her half what I earned at the shop. So I had 30 shillings a week which wasn't bad. I clothed myself with it. I bought my first lipstick, Yardley lipstick, that was great.

Lily's life was complicated by the fact that she was classified as a student on a special visa. But she was not going to school. Her uncle had made an arrangement with the nuns at Saint Monica's, a Catholic school in Cairns. He donated to the church and Lily had one afternoon each week of special lessons. After Lily came back from Melbourne her uncle made her contribute five shillings a week to her 'fees'. Each term the school signed the required papers for Lily's special visa. She learnt some bookkeeping, some typing, a bit of drafting, some sewing and a little English. And the Church added to its collection.

With Australia's White Australia Policy in place from Federation the population of Chinese-born rapidly declined. Between the 1890s and 1950s the numbers of Australian settlers born in China diminished by around 80 per cent to fewer than 7000. Newcomers were restricted to temporary visas so long term settlement would be prevented. However, those who remained were not so easily defeated. Lily's story shows that even law-abiding citizens like the nuns at Saint Monica's in Cairns could ignore the purification edicts of White Australia. These pockets of personal acceptance, sometimes encouraged by small financial deals, helped families like Lily's circumvent the immigration bars.

The push for a 'European', or more accurately a non-Asian, Australia began its popular appeal not in extremist conservative movements but in radical writings such as the pro-nationalist outpourings in *The Bulletin* of the 1880s. The nascent trade union movement and Australian Labor parties were also in the forefront of the nudge to 'whiten' the colonies. In the 1890s, as Andrew Markus points out in *Fear*

& *Hatred*, the unions' obsessive proselytising did dissipate a little which led some to protest, like the writer in the Sydney *Worker* in 1899, that 'the public unfortunately are very apathetic'[4] about White Australia. But opposition to non-Europeans persisted in trade union circles, especially in the Australian Workers Union (strong in Queensland) which cheered for White Australia long into the twentieth century. And it was not until Donald Horne took over as editor of *The Bulletin* in 1961 that its slogan 'Australia for the Whiteman' was removed from the masthead.

Support for White Australia, however, did increasingly come from a disparate group as the policy was enforced. When immigration became a focus, with the *Empire Settlement Act 1922* and the 'Dreadnought Boys' schemes, calls for a European Australia, preferably one populated with fair-skinned Brits, became the preoccupation of many conservative groups as well. Percy Stephensen's eccentric *The Foundations of Culture in Australia*, published in 1936, best illustrates the confused ideological base of White Australia. Stephensen, a Queenslander, was an early member of the Australian Communist Party who ended up being interned during World War II as a supporter of Fascism. His move from left to right had little impact, however, on his fundamental belief in a European Australia. In *The Foundations of Culture in Australia* he is pugnacious in defence of an 'Australian' nationality as opposed to an 'Imperial' one of slavishness to Britain. But the national culture he envisages is 'white' and derived from mother Britain and he sees the expanding population in Australia as 'the future home of the white race'.[5]

Out beyond the fringes of this official and intellectual opposition to non-European settlement and woven into the small business communities of major towns a network of Asian or Chinese support structures survived. It was a semi-fugitive existence.

Our status was terrible then. Everyone seemed to be on a temporary visa. You got an extension every six months if they liked you. If they didn't out you went. You needed someone to give a guarantee and then they would stamp your visa. If the family had a business like mine or my ex-husband's family then sometimes you got a twelve

*months extension. The Immigration Department went
around knocking on doors all the time to find illegal
immigrants.*

At the forefront of pressure to retain White Australia in
the postwar years was the Australian Labor Party. James Jupp,
in *Arrivals and Departures*, makes the often forgotten point
that in the 1950s Liberal Ministers for Immigration like Harold
Holt became aware of the interests of manufacturers in wid-
ening the immigration intake. Manufacturers argued that
British immigration could not adequately supply the need for
labour in Australia. But pressure from ALP members like
Leslie Haylen, whose lavish praise of Mao's China is contained in his book *Chinese Journey*, continued to hound the
conservative government over any sign that White Australia
might be relaxed. Such Labor members were maintaining the
sentiments of Arthur Calwell, Immigration Minister in the
Chifley Government, who in November 1946 expressed the
hope that, with the expanded postwar immigration programs,
'for every foreign migrant there will be ten people from the
United Kingdom'.[6] Lily's family had little time for Mr Calwell.
His policies meant immigrants like Lily's father in Melbourne
needed to keep their heads down.

As a community Lily's family and friends were great survivors. Squeezed between the endless hours of work there
were good times. It is still Lily's knack to wrest delicious fun
from a working week and as I listen to her story we are
munching on gow gee, tiny Chinese pasties straight from her
elaborate kitchen steamer, and freshly made dim sims whose
texture and flavour would challenge any Chinese chef. Back
in 1952 Lily could manage similar tricks of pleasure from the
cinders. In Melbourne she fitted in an energetic social life
before being packed off back to Cairns. Her stepmother did
not want Lily but she was happy to offer entertainment while
Lily was in her care. They went to restaurants and parties
and Lily credits her with being the person who taught her
how to eat out, how to order and how to behave with style;
in Lily's words 'the good life'. She also remembers having
three boyfriends. One came to pick her up for dates in his
father's Pontiac, one was a taxi driver and one was a friend
she met on the boat coming to Australia.

Ronald with the Pontiac met Lily through a small 'salon'

circle that gathered at the terraced home of an aunt. Looking back Lily realised that aunty was matchmaking for some of the young local Chinese men who were encouraged to look Lily over as a prospective bride. The Chinese-born population was dwindling in Australia and this meant there was a decreasing number of young Chinese women available to marry. Many local Chinese men had to be content with non-Chinese brides. As a result of aunty's matchmaking Lily remembers a night with Ronald at the Dragon Ball as the highlight of her time in Melbourne.

I didn't have a dress and my father wouldn't give me any money. I borrowed a dress from Aunty Gladys, my stepmother's sister. She was about three times my size. So I got a big belt and pulled it all in and didn't look too bad. It was a cold night and everyone was in their furs. I had a black cardigan over a pink dress. But it was lovely. Ronald was the first man who gave me a corsage.

In the Australia of the 1990s it is hard to imagine a Chinese community cut off from its traditional cuisine in any sense. Chinatowns in every major city centre provide an infinite variety of Chinese foodstuffs and the Chinese restaurant is as common as fish and chip shops. But in the early 1950s Lily went back to Cairns with her head full of Chinese recipes her relatives had never tasted. Lily's aunt in Cairns was a good cook. She could make a fruit cake with no recipe, filling her mixing bowl Chinese style with handfuls of ingredients— using her instinct to measure the quantities needed. Uncle could cook well too. On Sundays the family sat down to his (English) Sunday roasts. Lily watched closely to learn for herself. Once or twice a week Lily was allowed to cook for the family. She loved the kitchen partly because it took her away from the shop, but she also enjoyed cooking.

After Melbourne and the 'good life' in restaurants and among Chinese settlers from a different part of China, Lily began serving the dishes she had seen and eaten in Melbourne. She gave her uncle's family chicken and sweet corn soup and they had never tried it. She cut the beans and carrots in a fancy way and she stir-fried the meat which they all thought wonderful. The insularity of her relatives' provincial village culture was quietly invaded by the tastes and fancies of a region further north, just south of Shanghai. The experience would probably not have been possible back in the China they had left with its distinct provinces and separate cultures. In a multicultural migrant setting provincial ways are quickly broken down.

In Cairns, by 1953, the small Chinese community had become an intrinsic and socially accepted part of the landscape, its prosperity contributing to local coffers. At a 1953 fund-raising beauty pageant in Cairns the judges selected Miss Italy for first prize, Miss China for second and Miss Germany for third. Lily was Miss China. A black and white photo in the family album pictures her catwalk appearance, a shapely black-haired girl in 1950s bathing costume (borrowed from a relative) walking on between a 4QY microphone and a stage wall hung with an enormous Australian flag. Against the flag and partly covering it is the larger-than-life portrait of the new monarch Queen Elizabeth II, gilt-framed and looking as if it has been removed from high up on the walls of the Lord Mayor's chambers.

When Lily finally married, officially she was only sixteen. In fact she was twenty. Her father gave permission, glad to be moving the responsibility to someone else who would supposedly keep and provide for Lily in the customary Chinese manner. Lily's letters had endlessly begged for more money and he had sent a couple of pounds every six months or so. Courting was strictly a family affair and aunty had ruled out visits from male friends beyond a total of three. Lily's chances at a love life were under lock and key.

Social occasions came after long working days. Other opportunities were parties organised by the various 'cousins' from Lily's village who had settled in Cairns. When Uncle Willie closed the shop at ten Lily, after serving a fourteen hour shift behind the counter, slipped off with her cousin Jessie for a few hours of dancing. Sometimes they were lucky and the uncle closed up at 8.30 pm. And there were lots of visitors from further afield, towns like Rockhampton and Townsville which are further south on Queensland's coastal fringe. Lily, who was pretty while her older cousin was plain, seemed to attract admirers easily. This did not please her aunt and uncle. When visitors had left after speaking well of the 'pretty' niece, aunty would become angry with Lily. It meant the only admirers who were safe to encourage were those, like the cast off clothes, not among Jessie's favourites.

Cobbled together from only a few meetings and very little time alone, Lily had begun a friendship with a man of 27 who had come to Australia just a month after she did. They had known one another since arriving in Cairns. He worked for his uncle who ran a general store, a shop that stocked everything like a mini-department store and stayed open all hours into the night. Eventually Lily agreed to marry him. Lily's choice of husband suited her aunt as he only had a temporary visa and was of no great interest because he had no money. The marriage must have seemed like a great escape to Lily but as things turned out she was in for another hard grind.

In 1991 a study of ethnic small business in the Chinese and Indian communities of Brisbane and Sydney, titled *Asian Entrepreneurs in Australia*, made a number of recommendations to the federal government. Among them was the suggestion that 'concessionary family reunion should be made easier for established independent business people who are prepared to employ . . . relatives'[7] and that a special category might be created to encourage migrants of this sort. What the study revealed was that many successful small businesses in Australia have been created out of the ability of Asian immigrants to transfer skills into select areas of trade and commerce by way of the family business. Often this was the result of discriminatory policies against overseas qualifications in the professions. At other times family businesses have been created out of maximum avoidance of the cost of employment.

There is no doubt that in Lily's and her husband's families there was clear illustration of the success of Asian entrepreneurs. Lily's father had worked up a successful business in Melbourne as had her uncle in Cairns. Her husband's uncle was also running a thriving business in Cairns. Their grocery businesses were dependent on Australian custom and did not simply spring out of supplying a readymade ethnic population.

Chinese food didn't exist in those days. Australians
wouldn't eat Chinese. And you couldn't get Chinese food.
You could cook Chinese style with vegetables but there

*were no traditional condiments and so on. My aunty had
to grow her own vegetables, but there were no Chinese
mushrooms or the seaweed. Sometimes when a boat came
in they would buy some off the seamen. My aunty got to
know the boats and was good at that.*

However, success in business was possible only when
husbands and wives became good partners and while the
male head of the family was a good businessman. In addition
it required absolute frugality and dedication over time to one
project. For Lily there was to be no long-lasting success story
with her marriage partner. Her husband proved to be the
weak link in the family business story. And Lily, like a good
Chinese wife, had to stand in his shadow no matter what
business acumen she might have herself.

They lost their first thousand pounds, borrowed from the
husband's uncle, in a hamburger shop. They worked till 2.00
am some nights trying to catch the movie crowd. When the
gas in the kitchen began to irritate Lily's husband he decided
to give the business away, asked the owner for his money
back and was refused. He walked out with nothing after
paying his uncle back. Lily was three months pregnant. They
headed for Sydney to look for work and stopped in Rockhampton when friends suggested the prospects were better
there. In Gladstone Road they opened a small grocery store
with the help of a loan of 200 pounds. Lily reels off the
incidents with increasing groans of irritation.

*We would buy a case of apples, a case of oranges and
ten pounds of bananas, sell them and then pay the
wholesaler. I suppose we were making a little and had
somewhere to live. Then Sandie was born in 1958. Just
before she was born and because he was trying to get
permanent residency my husband had to go for a
medical check-up. They told him he had TB. He was in
hospital for six months. There I was with a new baby,
one week old, a business to run and a husband in a
house in the country twenty miles out of Rockhampton.*

Lily kept the shop open, faint with hunger in the afternoons because she had no time to cook. She had a friend
who sometimes brought a chicken that she cut up in pieces
to last the week. Soon after Sandie was born Lily found she

was unable to nurse the baby adequately and had to leave her at the hospital until she was feeding better. Some Australian neighbours stepped in to help mind the shop. And Lily struggled on—with a little help from her friends as the saying goes.

Attitudes to the White Australia Policy were changing. The *Migration Act 1958* abolished the notorious dictation test which had been used to exclude non-European applicants, and also removed references to race or nationality in the legislation. There was still the need for an entry permit and these were given at the discretion of the Minister and the public servants who ran the department. A lot of screening out of Asian applicants could continue and it did. A year earlier the government had passed legislation to allow permanent residence to non-Europeans of good character who had been in Australia for at least fifteen years. Lily's husband did not qualify because he had been a resident for less than eight years, but the news of the relaxation of official policy encouraged him to make early moves to shrug off his temporary status. It was not until 1967 that Lily and her husband were naturalised, at the first opportunity.

In the Australian community, even in conservative Rockhampton in conservative Queensland, attitudes also were becoming more tolerant. Lily's friends were not just Chinese. They were a mixture of locals, customers mainly, who realised the young Chinese shopkeeper was having a hard time. Lily even had medical insurance before her baby was born, invested in after a visit from a local salesman who explained the benefits. He advised a cheap rate, one that did not pay for her confinement but which was a lifeline when her baby became ill. Rockhampton was a small community and everyone helped. Some of the Chinese 'cousins' took turns to look in and help. An elderly Australian couple who lived across the street with a vintage car and a gracious home that Lily thought of as a palace dropped in morning and night. An Indian who worked as a storeman for the grocery distributor helped to put away the stock and check the shelves. Others came in to buy especially from Lily to help boost her trade—eggs, milk, bread, whatever. Some even helped to bath the baby when there were customers to serve. Lily remembers them all very fondly. But when her husband

came out of the sanatorium the props disappeared. Again
Lily's husband proved a weak business partner and the shop
had to be abandoned. So they moved on.

Some bleaker times followed, survived when Lily found
work as a waitress in Brisbane. Eventually they were able to
make a fresh start with borrowed capital. A friend in the
Brisbane Chinese community, who was wealthy enough to
own property, went guarantor for the loan. It was 1963. So
Lily and her husband started the first Chinese restaurant in
Southport. They called it the Oriental and for many years it
changed very little in appearance, as Lily discovered on a
return visit thirty years later. When Lily and her husband
opened the Southport restaurant her father, who had left his
second wife, had begun another restaurant on the Gold Coast
at Mermaid Beach. Lily's husband worked briefly with him
before starting the Oriental with Lily. But the venture was
short-lived.

So we worked there for about a year. Then he started
again. He got sick, he complained about the work and he
would not let me get a cook. With a cook I could have
carried on because I was making money. But he was in
control of the money. The trouble was he liked to put the
money in his pocket. Bills weren't paid. People were
ringing up for their money. The business was in my
name and I should have been ruthless. I should have
kicked him out and carried on the business without him.
I managed before. The money just went. He went
bankrupt.

Lily could have got rid of her husband and started afresh
but she resisted, letting conservative patterns rule. Submission
was her practice and had been for too long. There were
opportunities to leave which, looking back with the wisdom
of fifty years Lily recognises a little wistfully. One wealthy
older man, who had made a fortune dealing in discounted
damaged groceries during the war, blew in to look her up
while she was struggling with the restaurant. He had come
by unannounced on other occasions over the years, offering
sympathy and flattery in the midst of the hardship. It was
tempting. In Southport he argued strongly that Lily should
leave and dared to recommend it in front of her husband

which caused further friction. But Lily stayed. At the end of eighteen months in the restaurant her husband was admitted to a clinic suffering a nervous breakdown.

In 1965 officialdom never considered how the migrant experience might be a cause of some mental disorder. Lily's husband had a low resistance to the abnormal trials associated with living as a temporary resident. He was probably irresponsible in many ways but his original culture and his adopted culture defined him as a failure. By the time he entered the clinic the Oriental had been sold.

Lily's husband underwent treatment and Lily kept the family. When the Oriental was sold she signed a 'goodwill' agreement that she would not open another restaurant in a nearby area. So she tried a fish and chips shop for a brief while in Brisbane and then a restaurant at Burleigh Heads. Sandie had a brief term as a boarder at Saint Hilda's in Southport where the girls claimed the headmistress's Pekinese dog ate better than the students. After her businesses proved poor income earners Lily moved to sales work in boutiques and eventually into a position at Myer Chermside. Applying for jobs at this time she found it was not unusual that employers would ask if she was Asian after they heard her voice on the phone. Those who did this let her know she need not apply. Still, life did begin to improve financially. Lily and her husband bought a house. Then suddenly, without explanation, Lily's husband decided the family should move to Sydney. Here was the real goldmine he told them and spoke glowingly of what fortune lay ahead.

In Sydney, however, it was no Gold Mountain as expected. Lily's husband spent most of his days and nights with friends in Chinatown, while at home he had little to share with his wife and daughter.

I took the first week of the school holidays off from work to spend with Sandie. I thought as a family we should get to know Sydney. I told my husband we might go around and look at the goldmine he had told us about. But he didn't want to go anywhere. We sat at home looking at one another. He didn't want to spend his money. I had to buy the food even. As time went by you couldn't say we were happy. When he was down I tried to talk to him. I was his wife, I was his manager, I was his money

*manager, I was his minder and I was his psychiatrist. I
said to him, 'Do something to escape. Go to the races. At
least if you lose money you will have done something'.*

Lily began to live with emotional blackmail too as her
husband threatened suicide. Yet it was years before she could
bring herself to leave. She had worked in Sydney from the
time she arrived and by then had an established group of
friends, mainly from Myer where she had become a beautician. Finally Lily decided to separate from her husband.

In 1973 the findings of the Immigration Family Survey
conducted by the Department of Immigration showed that
twice as many migrant families would be in poverty if the
wife was not working, principally as a result of the inade-
quate primary income earned by the male breadwinner—an
inadequacy due to lack of skills or skills conversion or ability
to communicate in English. The report drew a picture of the
difficulties a migrant family had to face in these circumstances. It criticised the Australian community for not
providing appropriate interpreting and communication services, in hospitals, courts or public services such as local
government, saying such lack compounded the migrant difficulties. All these factors had certainly been present in Lily's
difficult life. However, in her divorce proceedings it became
clear that the family should not have been so poor at all.
Lily's husband, who had eventually found work in Sydney as
a chef, had been squirrelling money away for his own use.
Their impoverishment was largely due to the fact that for
years they had chiefly lived on Lily's modest take-home pay.

The separation agreement gave Lily $17 000. Her solicitor
advised her to settle out of court. It was no grand sum after
a quarter of a century of hard work, frugality and sacrifice.
With the savings she had scraped together from her salary it
bought her a unit in Bankstown and she furnished it by
working weekends at the Big Wheel Hotel nearby, catering
and doing any odd jobs to be found about the hotel. Her
husband had enough money left after the settlement to buy
a beautiful tenth floor apartment in more select Artarmon.
Sandie chose to go with her father and nowadays candidly
admits to wanting to exploit her father's sudden wealth for
all she could. While he was away she had a luxury pad to
herself. Lily started out on her own in Bankstown with the

money from her marriage settlement. As a naturalised Australian she could buy property and she needed only a very small mortgage.

In Lily's Bankstown unit the rooms ascend with mezzanine floors on five levels in an uncommon, almost oriental, use of vertical space. Our lunch in the dining room is on the first level overlooking the ground floor sitting room, and adjacent to the kitchen. Above on separate levels are three more rooms and a second bathroom. We finish the interview hearing accounts of Maurice's first visit to Lily's unit at the end of an evening out. Living alone Lily was taking no chances with male visitors she had known for such a brief time. So she spun a tale that her grandmother was sleeping upstairs and said they had to be quiet so as not to wake her. Listening to her very workaday girlfriends Lily had been regaled with stories of mass prejudice about the horrors of ethnic boyfriends.

I told him not to make too much noise because my grandmother was sleeping upstairs. He has never forgotten that. I thought, I don't know him. He could be a murderer for all I knew. And before this I used to hear so much from one of my Australian girlfriends. She used to say Italians, Yugoslavs, Greeks, Lebanese and so on were all horrible, vicious and violent. And now I was sitting at home late at night with a Lebanese man I hardly knew. So eventually Maurice left and had to wait for his friend outside. And he waited for hours because his friend didn't turn up till one o'clock in the morning.

In Sydney Lily and Maurice exemplify a multicultural experience fast invading Australia's most multicultural city. Half of Lily's contacts and family are traditional Chinese. When Maurice's family doctor suggested surgery to cure an eye complaint Lily took Maurice to a Chinese herbalist in Sussex Street near the city's Chinatown. The herbalist fixed the eye and added a complete physical overhaul of massage and purgatives. Maurice felt sick for days and then emerged as fit as a dragon. Lily has a lot of relatives and friends in Sydney and they shop and eat regularly in Chinatown, now a ritzy tourist showpiece backing on to the Entertainment Centre and lit by neon signs around its huge shopping malls and retail outlets. Some have businesses there. These days Lily also shops in Bankstown where an influx of Chinese and Vietnamese has transformed the poorer side of the railway line into a cosmopolitan market town. Here Lily buys her Chinese herbs and vegetables, the wong buck or Chinese cabbage, the buck choy with its turnip-like white tubes and leaves, the green and yellow choy sum for stir fry, green ginger, green pawpaws for soup, dried mushrooms and dried squid, lotus nuts, wheat starch and sticky rice flours, and red bean paste and lotus root for sweet dishes.

On the other side of Lily's family and friendship the network is quite diverse. There are Lebanese relatives with some Syrian intermarriage and there is the Italian family of her son in law. When Maurice met Lily he was out with his karate club friends who were Malayan. Workmates who have remained close can be anything. In Tenille, Lily's granddaughter, lies the future. Like Jenny Kee in *The Coming Republic* who says, 'I am the future . . . an example of what Australia is going to become. Half European, half Asian'.[8]

When I interviewed Lily she had been a beautician at David Jones in Bankstown for thirteen years, winning trips to Port Douglas, Hong Kong and Hawaii in successive years for her selling efforts. And she still has friends from Myer. Her workmates, from all types of backgrounds, were her support when her marriage ended.

We had good times. Joanne was English, Edna Australian, Denise was Italian and Kath and Sandra were Australian. Violet was Greek. They invited me to their places and I invited them back to mine. And I remember when I moved into my unit I didn't have much and I asked the girls over for dinner. Violet said, 'Look you're working, so we'll all bring a plate'. When Maurice started to come out with me they brought their husbands and we had some great times.

Lily is an enigma as a national statistic, as are many of her relatives, especially her father who celebrated his eighty-first birthday in Brisbane in 1992. In the period when Arthur Calwell was Immigration Minister a burst of antagonism against non-Europeans was unleashed by the Immigration Department. Deportations of the non-European spouses of

Australians became the most notorious manifestation of Arthur Calwell's dictates. He railed against this 'thin edge of the wedge' that would undermine White Australia. As A.C. Palfreeman points out in *The Administration of the White Australia Policy*, most of the cases that gave Arthur Calwell such a bad name were cases of deportation which separated husbands, wives and children. Throughout this period Lily's father was a prime target, yet he avoided suspicion.

Lily also defies classification, like many who live in the gaps in the official statistics. Australia's White Australia Policy forced families into subterfuge in the face of tightly policed restrictions. In 1954 the Census indicated that there were 1506 Chinese-born females in Australia. Immigration Department figures, however, showed only 339 who had legal exemption certificates. In 1966 the number of full Chinese with permanent residence in Australia was only 7400. At the same time there were 8500 temporary resident Chinese, almost all of whom were students.

Somewhere in that bundle of official statistics was Lily who was neither permanent resident nor student, but who had gained entry on a student visa in 1951. Her expectations on leaving Hong Kong were quite illusory. Her achievements in Australia are still hard to quantify. But Lily has conquered the Gold Mountain, getting a little bruised along the way and finishing the trail with her financial fortune still extremely modest. And like many thrust into surviving as immigrants Lily has surpassed her origins in so many ways. Evaluating the experience she says, with a little pleasure, 'I've done everything. You name it, I did it'.

Judy

WHEN I rang my friend Judy to discuss the interview she was struggling with her latest creation. It was called 'God Playing Dice with Alice in Quantum Wonderland' and it was taking shape on canvas in her downstairs studio. I could sense it wasn't going to be an easy birth.

In Judy's 'God and Alice' painting, as in most of her paintings, you can find particles of the whole Judy. She once wrote to me, 'Everything fits into a marvellous jigsaw in my life and sometimes I get a wonderful inkling of the wholeness of it all'. Without drawing breath her next sentence was, 'I'll need $1500 to stage it. . .'.

Judy is a rare combination of rigorous self-discipline and intuitive, exuberant self-expression. Her tall energetic frame is topped with a mass of thick, tightly formed black curls which she controls as soon as they are washed rather than allow any chaotic bushiness. Her dark eyes are windows on a passionate soul, excited always about fresh discoveries and new insights. Her smile is intense. At times it becomes her way of willing positive thinking and ebullient optimism. The fact that her star sign is Scorpio is not surprising.

When Judy wrote to me about the '$1500', she was referring to the amount needed to stage an exhibition of her work at the Roar 2 Gallery in Brunswick Street, Fitzroy, during the cold of July and August in recession-wracked Melbourne, with part of the proceeds going to Austcare. The exhibition, however small in the congested world of the connoisseur, represented Judy's first real break as an artist and to get there she was investing her own money on the rent for the two weeks, the invitations and the publicity, giving half of the profits away and hoping for a little recognition. But Judy was on cloud nine.

She called the exhibition 'The Cosmic Dance'. The catalogue listed 42 paintings with titles like, 'Fibonacci Spirals with Green Harmony', 'Oh Jerusalem', 'Jupiter, the Bringer of Jollity', 'I'm Stuck on Mathematics', 'The Joy of Feynman Diagrams' and 'The Clockwork Universe'. And she made a profit. Even better, Judy was still on cloud nine afterwards. A call from the organisers of a concert connecting art and science, and hosted by ABC personality Phillip Adams in the Adelaide Town Hall, had confirmed her recognition. The renowned scientist Paul Davies, author of *The Mind of God* and *God and The New Physics*, who was addressing the function wanted to make use of her paintings for his talk. Did she have any slides they asked. Yes she did. Another twirl in Judy's cosmic dance was under way.

Self-taught in her painting Judy has developed her style by grabbing at her life experience of over fifty years. In a labour camp at three having missed the train to Auschwitz Judy has lived through escape, refugee camps, resettlement in Australia, convent life, a happy marriage and scrupulous hard work. Her two great obsessions, science and a belief in God, drive her inspiration. Exploring 'new age' books like those of Paul Davies, the scientist searching for 'ultimate meaning', adds further dimensions to the jigsaw. Put it all together and the result is best described by Judy herself.

I just finished 'Saturn, the Bringer of Old Age'. The music suggests figures struggling, dragging themselves up a

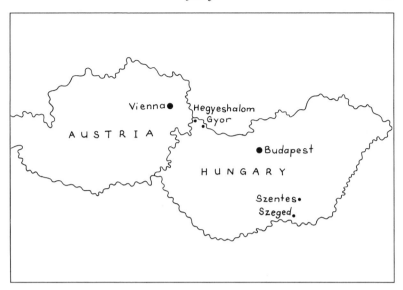

crystal mountain, the bells of a church ringing and dark purple clouds above them in an orange sky. The painting has a slightly cubist air, the crystals of the mountain glitter in shades of grey-blue, the stylised figures are quite powerful but heavy. It was so difficult to get the crystals right, but I did it.

On my first meeting with Judy in early 1967 I was immediately struck by her positive zeal. Next to my self-deprecating manner, Judy's enthusiasm is sometimes scary. Nonetheless it is the key to her survival. That summer Judy married Joe. She was 26 and only halfway through her Science degree at Melbourne University, with two more years before it would be complete. Already after just a quarter of a century Judy had chalked up quite a lot of memorable experiences.

Joe and Judy both came to Australia from Hungary after the 1956 revolution. But they didn't know one another then. As a child Judy had grown up in Szentes, a town in the south of Hungary. Her family was middle class, owning a newsagency or paper shop, which her mother was to inherit after her grandfather died during the war.

During the war Judy's father went away to wartime service. As a Jew he became part of an outcast unit given suicidal tasks like picking up mines. Few of his unit survived.

In Szentes, in May 1944, Judy and her mother were rounded up with other Jewish families and taken to a camp in Szeged some miles south of Szentes. From there they were herded in freight train wagons towards Auschwitz.

Every time I see a cattle train I think of it. My mother and I were destined to go to Auschwitz with a group of Hungarian people that were her close friends. She desperately wanted to go with them. But because I was asleep she had to look for me and their train was full by the time she got me. She could not get on. She went up and down the train to make sure she could get a place but all the doors were shut. The train went and we were on the next one. By the time our train got to a certain junction, the railway line had been bombed, probably by the Americans, I don't know, and it couldn't continue towards Poland. We were diverted to Austria.

For a chilling and graphic (half a sentence) reminder of what the Hungarian mother and daughter escaped by not going to Auschwitz in mid-1944, read page 137 of Martin Amis' novel *Time's Arrow*. Instead, Judy and her mother spent the last year or so of the war in a labour camp near Vienna and Judy's mother, who spoke fluent French, managed to have what Judy describes as a 'marvellous love affair' by talking through the wire with a Frenchman who made up poems for her.

For the years I have known Judy there is a barely visible scar of shame in her small experience of the holocaust. Discussion is tempered, excused and, if you know her well, you will see that she freezes a little, inwardly startled by a little collapse, then picking up confidently she moves herself on to make sure it won't happen again.

As the Third Reich of Hitler's Germany disintegrated the Russians came and Judy and her mother were 'liberated'. After the war Judy's parents divorced and Judy remembers standing at the front gate at the age of five and announcing proudly to the neighbourhood, 'We have divorced'. Undaunted, Judy's mother took the quite common step of advertising for a companion. (In Australian Hungarian newspapers such advertisements are still popular.) Mother remarried one of the applicants, who treated Judy well until her new brother was born whereafter she fell, as she puts it, 'from the state of grace'.

Judy's mother meanwhile had become a devoted Communist believing the party was the way to social justice. She obediently 'offered' her shop to the state when asked to do so, although this meant the family lost their livelihood in Szentes. They sold up their house and moved to Budapest where they rented a flat, paying the customary 'key money' for their right to occupy. Judy's mother went to work in a factory, attended meetings of the Communist Party and Judy's stepfather went back to work in his trade as a printer. But tension developed as the small nest egg from the sale of the house in Szentes dwindled. Judy's mother eventually chose divorce a second time. Mother and daughter were by then on the brink of dire poverty.

With the increasing hardship of daily life the Communist system was starting to appear somewhat disillusioning for Judy's mother. The social justice she had expected was not forthcoming. The jails were filling with those who voiced dissent or represented class enemies, the countryside had been chaotically collectivised and there was little sign of benefit to workers from increased industrial production. In fact the standard of living for average Hungarians was diminishing rapidly. When Judy's mother voiced her misgivings that practice was falling far short of the 'ideals of Lenin' she found herself expelled from the party. She joined many others like her. Simultaneously Judy was falling in love at the age of thirteen—with physics.

A young teacher had Judy spellbound.

She became my godmother eventually, because through her teaching I fell in love with physics. I used to run after her after school classes and ask her all sorts of penetrating questions. And when we were studying gravity and these wondrous forces of the universe eventually I got to the ultimate question—what makes it tick? And she risked jail and persecution to say to me, 'Some people call it nature, other people call it God'.

Judy had never known religious belief of any kind. Her family were atheists and she attended local state-run schools. Till then she had been very proud of her independent thinking, free of props like religious belief—the opium of the people as she had been taught. The physics teacher opened a new world for Judy who now looked around for a group of believers she could join. 'The only people who gave me definite answers were the Catholics', says Judy. And adds quickly, 'Quite different from nowadays'.

Judy became a Catholic exactly a year before the outbreak of the Hungarian Revolution and a week before her fifteenth birthday. She was baptised in a small chapel in Budapest. Her step was a courageous one. There would be little future in physics for the daughter of an expelled party member who had decided to become a Catholic. She would never be allowed to study at university. She would be classified down. But once again Judy's optimism prevailed.

At home, life with mother was deteriorating. Judy confesses to being a very critical, if not difficult, adolescent. Charged with her twin beliefs in physics and God she went along to the Education Ministry and begged, pleaded and cajoled for permission to go to boarding school where she could study her physics seriously, away from home distractions. Judy got her wish. There would be no relinquishing of her new religious convictions either. At the boarding school Judy found a way to sneak out and join other Catholics for Mass. When she was discovered it further marked her out in the eyes of her teachers. She was an oddball, a religious fanatic and also unruly. Then the revolution came.

A series of leadership changes had been unsettling Hungarian politics since the death of Stalin in 1953. Hungary's hardline leader Matyas Rakosi, with his devotion to a Moscow line, had been replaced by Imre Nagy in July 1953. Nagy was a strong party man but seen as 'Hungarian' in his basic attitudes. Some reforms were begun and he promised the release of political prisoners, an end to the practice of forcing farmers into collectives and an end to forced development of heavy industry. But in 1955 Moscow dismissed Nagy and installed a succession of strong 'Moscow' leaders. Nagy was expelled from the party.

Then suddenly in 1956 the earlier reforms of Nagy, the 'secret speech' of Nikita Khrushchev denouncing Stalin and the Polish uprising all combined to trigger a fresh spirit in Hungary. A student protest march in Budapest on 23 October set out to present a petition for reforms. When police fired on the students it became the beginning of a bloody revolution.

Judy remembers how at first it was glorious to hear that 'freedom' had arrived. Their joy was short-lived when the Hungarian secret police turned on the protestors and the shooting started. Judy was with the first surge of crowds near the radio station.

I never had a chance to stay even if I wanted to. We were just swept away and the next lot of people took our places. So many people were killed. The next day we heard that in front of the parliament there was a terrible massacre. They just shot into the crowd. . . A few days later the Russians came in. Tanks were shooting into houses. The walls of three and four storey blocks were shot away and people's lives were just sort of hanging out, shot to pieces.

The Hungarian political situation seesawed for a couple of weeks between Hungarian victory and Russian dominance. For a while the Hungarian Army and the student protesters were thought to have won through as the Russian tanks retreated to just over the border and a government of factions was assembled under Imre Nagy. Cardinal Jozsef Mindszenty was escorted from his prison to his bishop's palace by a cheering crowd. Members of the State Security Department were forced to flee. But the concessions made to Nagy's pluralist ruling body eventually became too much for Moscow to tolerate especially when Nagy announced Hungary's withdrawal from the Warsaw Pact on 1 November. By 4 November the Russian tanks were well in control of Budapest again, Nagy was sheltering in the Yugoslavian Embassy and Cardinal Mindszenty was in hiding with the American Legation. In time Nagy would be abducted to Romania. Later he was tried and executed.

For a while Judy sheltered with her mother in the cellar of a hospital where her mother worked. She still remembers one fourteen year old boy badly wounded in the groin. 'I am pretty sure he would have died. He was so frail and weak and I just saw the revolution personalised in him', recalls Judy.

By December it was evident that there was absolutely no hope that a new order would be formed out of the revolution. Judy talked to her mother and they decided to make a run for the border. They took nothing but what they wore as so many in their position have done before and after them. They bought tickets to Gyor, halfway between Budapest and Vienna. They planned to stay on the train till it crossed the Austrian border. With the revolution the borders were still open; it was their only chance. However, at the border town of Hegyeshalom they and about thirty others were taken by the guards and locked up in a watch house.

Being confined in the hut made the situation desperate till, on pure instinct using a ploy she cannot remember, Judy managed to get outside, her thin body swollen with the layers of her entire wardrobe. In the freezing air, with measured pleading, she started to work on one of the young men who was armed and keeping watch. He told her he had orders to shoot if anyone tried to escape. She told him that life was not worth living if she could not leave what had become a police state. Then Judy sensed his reluctance and made a chance move.

I felt that he liked me. And after a while, instead of walking back and forth, I just kept walking. I knew from the direction of the train which way was west, so I kept walking that way. He didn't shoot me. So I walked across . . . it was a lovely, snowy, clear night. Everything was covered with snow except the train lines . . . by New Year's Eve I was in Vienna.

In Vienna Judy discovered that her mother had also escaped. She had climbed out a window of the hut. Obviously the guards could not cope or they simply didn't want to. Judy's mother had found her daughter by asking endlessly at refugee centres till someone answered to Judy's description. Once she knew her daughter was safe the mother, ever practical, suggested that they go their separate ways. They would each be better off as single women; she to marry again, Judy to find a refugee passage to somewhere safe. Elsewhere in Hungary Joe had also walked out, leaving everything except one roast duck to eat on the way. By the end of the revolution 200 000 Hungarians had escaped Communist Hungary. On 8 November an Australian newspaper reported that 10–15 000 had been killed and 50 000 wounded in the fighting that had followed the Hungarian uprising.

The bloodshed and terror in Hungary had captured the world's attention at a time when hostilities were under way in Suez and the Olympic Games were about to commence in Melbourne, Australia. Ironically the only other rival for Australian newspaper space at the time was Professor Sydney Sparkes Orr's appeal against dismissal by the University of Tasmania for having had an improper relationship with a young female student, the intrinsic details of which were faithfully reported each day in *The Age* through October and half of November.

As the Olympic torch arrived in Sydney on 18 November 40 000 people lined the route from Hornsby in the northern suburbs to the Town Hall entrance in George Street to watch its arrival. Australia was in international mode as its infant television stations opened their studios and Melbourne welcomed competitors from around the world to the Olympic Village in Heidelberg.

The 91-member Hungarian team arrived a week late and was greeted at Melbourne airport by 1200 emotional Hungarian-born Australians on 12 November. Three weeks later, in the closing days of the Games, the champion Hungarian water-polo team would create a sensation in a match against the Russians (Soviet Union). A whole 30 metres behind play Hungarian Ervin Zodar would come under attack from a Russian opponent and require several stitches to his eye. The Hungarians would win the match four goals to one and be cheered off while the crowd would boo and hiss at the Russians. In the same final days of competition the Australian Government would receive many applications from members of visiting teams like Hungary's requesting permission to stay in Australia.

Leading Australian figures responded relatively quickly to the Hungarian situation. Dr Daniel Mannix, Catholic Archbishop of Melbourne, condemned the Russian stranglehold on Hungary when addressing 500 railway employees on 28 October. On the previous night a large number of Hungarian-born Australians had marched to Melbourne's parliament to demonstrate their solidarity with the students of Budapest.

Soon after, Immigration Minister Athol Townley announced that Australia would take up to 3000 of the many Hungarians made victims by the Russian invasion. The government made a grant of £30 000 to Hungarian relief. In a speech to open the Wentworth by-election in Sydney on 15 November, Labor leader Dr H.V. Evatt felt the need to claim that nobody had condemned Russian action in Hungary more than he. Then, in the words which followed, he substantially compromised his stand against the Russians by equating their actions in Hungary with those of the British and French in Suez, where hostilities had begun against Egypt following President Nasser's annexation of the Suez Canal.

By the time Judy surfaced in Vienna the international relief effort was well under way. Conditions in the refugee centres were cramped and chaotic but there was food, freedom and the chance of a fresh home somewhere. Refugee centres were crowded sleeping quarters where male and female youngsters slept side by side in rooms containing fifty or sixty people. Judy was put between two boys and she remembers it taught her very quickly how to dress and undress under the cover of her clothes.

In the refugee centre, enduring these quite primitive circumstances, many soon found a lot could be traded by moving from bed to bed. On the way out to Australia Judy was the only girl of her age not pregnant. For these girls, early experiences of Australia included time spent in homes for unmarried mothers such as that run by the Josephite sisters in Broadmeadows, Melbourne.

My question by now is unavoidable—why did Judy choose Australia? And her answer is frank and exhibits a mixture of the youth she was and a maturity formed by early hardship.

Originally I wanted to go to Paris to the Sorbonne and follow in the footsteps of Madam Curie. But I found that in France the only way a young girl could make a living was to become a prostitute. And it did not fit in with my new religious convictions. So I looked for another country where with decent work I could earn enough to put myself through university. . . Canada and Australia would be the two countries.

When Judy chose Australia she went along to the Australian Embassy to apply. She was gruffly told the quota was full which appalled her. Surely one more wouldn't make much difference. The official replied that that was what everyone said. But Judy was not giving up having come this far.

I was alone and I wanted to come to Australia and he wouldn't let me. So I went day after day and he wouldn't let me fill out the forms or anything. One morning I got there at about seven o'clock and about ten o'clock, still hanging about, I saw this tea lady taking a tray to the inner office. . . I slipped in with her and turned on the tears and begged and pleaded, saying there was someone in Australia I loved and I wanted to follow him . . . they gave me a form to fill in and from then on it went very smoothly.

A few months later Judy left a hostel in Salzburg where she had remained waiting for her papers to be processed and a little later embarked on a Dutch ship from Rotterdam headed for Australia. The upheaval in the Suez Canal meant they took the longer route around South Africa. Their first stop in Australia was Fremantle where a priest interviewed each of the émigrés under eighteen to make an assessment of the most appropriate environment each could be placed in. Australian families had volunteered to foster young refugee arrivals like these. Most of the boys were sent to farming families in Tasmania, but Judy went on to Melbourne where she was to meet her second mother or, as Judy has always called her, 'mummy'. Meanwhile Judy's natural mother had found a new home in Israel.

The outpouring of literature in recent decades about personal experiences in Catholic institutions has not been generally complimentary in explaining the mores of religious life in Australia before the 1960s. Plays like *The Christian Brother*, television series like *The Leaving of Liverpool* and stories like *The Devil's Playground* tend to portray the imprint of the Catholic religious in the lives of the young through various psychotic stereotypes. Whether this is because those who have been badly affected by their experiences at school or in religious orders are more likely to write up those experiences is not something that can be assessed here.

However, in Judy's story of her early life in Australia there is a flip-side, and like all flip-side tunes it is not often heard.

Father Kevin Toomey, a Catholic priest from the Melbourne archdiocese, met Judy's group from Fremantle when it arrived in Melbourne. He was co-ordinating a relief depot at St Francis church in Lonsdale Street, especially set up to handle donations for the cause of Hungarian refugees. His role was to help settle the younger refugees in homes that had been allotted to them. The young new arrivals spent their first night at a temporary shelter in a former army camp in Broadmeadows. The following day Father Toomey took them all sight-seeing. Among the places of sacred importance to Melbournians he pointed out two great centres of worship— the Melbourne Cricket Ground and St Patrick's Cathedral. Then he introduced Judy to the family who had 'adopted' her.

Mrs Hughes' family lived in Kew and would most appropriately be described as quintessentially middle class Catholic Australia. At the time she was bringing up her daughters alone. One daughter, Vi, had just married so there was room in her household for another girl. Australian parish churches had encouraged families to help with the flood of refugees from the Hungarian disaster. Adopting Judy was Mrs Hughes' response. She was a lady who did a lot of helping out, driving the nuns around and other good works. Judy saw herself as a very special good work.

The three Hughes girls had gone to school at the Academy in Fitzroy. But Judy spoke little English and Mrs Hughes thought a school closer to home would be better. The closest Catholic convent school was Genazzano in Cotham Road, run by the FCJ sisters just around the corner. But in those days Genazzano was very exclusive. Mrs Hughes was told there was no room at the Genazzano inn. So Judy went to Siena Convent run by the Dominicans, a little further away in Camberwell but not too far.

Siena prided itself on its attention to academic merit. Judy had landed in a milieu she had once only dreamed of. Sister Carmel Leavey who was principal at the time remembers meeting Judy in the convent parlour the day Mrs Hughes brought her to Siena. 'I can still see that forlorn, dark and thin Hungarian girl with very little English standing with the lady who brought her.' Sister Carmel became an important mentor for Judy. 'A kinship developed over time that was partly academic and partly maternal', says Sister Carmel, who placed Judy in her own English and religion classes.

Opposite the convent in Riversdale Road and separated from it by the tracks of the city to Wattle Park trams is the Dominican Priory for priests. Next to the Priory is the imposing bluestone church of St Dominic that dominates the horizon for miles around. One of the priests at the Priory was Father Fazokas who was Hungarian and he was able to assist in working out what level of studies Judy could begin. She agreed to study Russian which she had also studied in Hungary. Finally Judy was put into Year 11. As with other children migrating Judy had hurdles to face that were immense. She remembers some of the first steps.

A third of the year gone, I took home my chemistry book, started from the word 'Preface' and looked up every word. Each day I wrote out fifty words in English and Hungarian and then Jan [Hughes] would read the English pronunciation for me and by the next day I would learn it. So in this way I could speak reasonably well and I understood everything. And I passed Leaving [Year 11] and then I passed Matriculation.

As she learnt English and succeeded in passing her exams where English was a compulsory subject Judy was made aware of the contrast her new life presented with her life in Hungary. She had never known people to be so good to her. For months she wondered what her new mother wanted from her in return, only to discover that Mrs Hughes and everyone helping her simply wanted her to succeed and be happy. Judy was not only learning English, chemistry and physics but she was becoming less cynical and very idealistic in response to the dedication of her new family and the nuns at Siena. She was also finding a whole new approach to the practice of her religion.

My practice of religion was not only allowed but even encouraged. I was confirmed while at Siena and the sister who prepared me spent many hours talking to me about the wonders of Christian doctrine which really thrilled me. I became a dedicated Christian. . . It was

*overwhelming that having read the gospels or the Song of
Songs I was sure I had a calling to be a nun.*

Father Fazokas, who had become a sort of spiritual adviser
as well as a help with the learning of English, did not think
Judy should rush into convent life. He advised her to go on
to university first and leave her decision till later. Others like
Sister Carmel recall that they had similar reservations. Judy
trusted Father Fazokas' wisdom and this caused what she
calls a crisis of conscience. Unable to know what to do she
decided to leave it to fate. If she won a Commonwealth
scholarship to university she would go to university. If she
did not she would become a Dominican nun. Judy missed
out on the scholarship.

The Dominican Order of nuns began its life in Australia
at Maitland in the Hunter Valley of New South Wales. A group
of nuns sent from the Cabra community in Dublin made up
the original foundation. In Continental Europe the life of the
Dominican nun had been monastic or enclosed for centuries.
But in Ireland things began to change. The needs of the
faithful were too great to ignore as successive waves of
anti-Catholic persecution denied the people their religion.
Throughout the penal times in Ireland groups of women from
many religious orders survived in back alleys and with the
help of families. They taught the children in spite of the risks
involved. The Cabra community was one of these and its
revolutionary stance meant it was logical that Dominican
nuns would continue their work among the many Irish
immigrants who had settled in New South Wales. From Maitland the order founded branch houses throughout eastern
Australia.

The strength of the Irish tradition in Australian Catholicism
grew out of the dominance in pure numbers of Irish Catholics
who made up Australian congregations in the first 150 years
of settlement. Dominance of ethnic numbers meant there was
an Irish-dominated clergy. The influx of wartime and postwar
migrants to Australia broadened the ethnic base in Australia,
especially after 1940. With it the population of the Australian
Catholic church began to change in composition and practice.
Whereas the religious institutes established up till 1900 had
been overwhelmingly Irish, the forty or so new religious
institutes of women established in Australia between 1946

and 1976 were mostly from southern and central Europe and a few from eastern Europe and Asia. At the same time the Catholic population more than doubled, a lot of it due to the large number of Catholics among postwar immigrants. But parish policy did not change. Catholic bishops left the Irish tradition well entrenched by marginalising migrant chaplains and hoping that newcomers would quickly assimilate in the parish schools. The effect was to alienate the children of migrant parents when they considered a future in religious life. By the 1960s as the Australian Catholic church was becoming multicultural, religious institutes, by comparison, remained mono-cultural.

When Judy joined the Dominicans there were around 13 000 women in religious life in Australia. Less than 15 per cent of them were overseas-born. She was well in the minority but she was certainly not alienated. In Sydney at 'Berith Park' in the North Shore suburb of Wahroonga Judy undertook her postulancy year and her one year as a novice. Today when she watches fictional recollections of convent life like *Brides of Christ* she becomes angry. *Ridiculous, ridiculous. There were no tensions there. The only thing that was important was to learn why the different rules exist and in what way they can help us to be closer to God.*

Judy does though admit to being on 'wings' saying, 'I had my head in the clouds; a lot of the other girls were not trying to keep the rules as rigorously'.

And Berith Park offered its own special balm in its leafy setting. Today the house is no longer owned by the Dominican order but it can be glimpsed through landscaped gardens from Billyard Avenue or the church grounds next door. Described as a 'landmark property' in a feature article in a Sydney newspaper in 1990, it occupies an acre or so of prime real estate in an area where many large gentrified gardens are the happy havens of the well off suburban professional. This is one of the suburbs described in Jessica Anderson's *The Impersonators* where 'spurs thrust into the bush as headlands do into the sea'.[1] Making use of the ideal location and leafy monastery-like grounds a number of Wahroonga's mansions have become institutions offering retreat, recuperation or instruction. In the days of Judy's novitiate the grounds of Berith Park were extensive, before the subdivider's pen marked out new lots. Judy remembers it as a wonderful place. The natural beauty of its mixture of European architecture and garden shrubs shaded by towering gums provided an arcadian setting for Judy's new understanding of biblical meaning.

We were learning the office and I became quite familiar with the Old Testament, the psalms and the rhythm of life—all in Latin. . . It was wonderful, the richness of it all and the strong connection between Judaism and Christianity struck me. . . It all hung together so beautifully. Even as an intellectual exercise it was beautiful but it was also a very deep emotional experience.

Incarcerated in Europe at the age of three for the crime of being Jewish, Judy was confronting for the first time a Jewish inheritance in a Catholic convent in Sydney in the language of the ancient Romans. It was a multicultural experience fit to shock Geoffrey Blainey.

A few novices left the ranks as time went by, discreetly. Anyone was free to go at any time. Most stayed. About twenty were professed after the two years. Days passed mostly in the silence of spiritual activity, listening to the novice mistress reading, singing the office and praying. Recreation times in set hours were riotously different. Judy remembers them putting on *HMS Pinafore* using their long calico aprons tied sideways over their legs to create sailors' pants. They put on *Everyman* and Judy mimed the part of Everyman, waving her arms about in a huge black cape, while someone read the words. At recreation Judy got a crash course in English literature.

But life inside the Dominican novitiate is just the precursor for good works beyond the walls. 'Faith without good works is dead' is an early dictum of the Catholic catechism. In her third year Judy began studying to become a primary school teacher. There was little training in the sense of present day college or university courses. It was made up of additional learning in amongst the regular novitiate program. The following year, as Sister Judith Maria, Judy began teaching classes at Santa Sabina in Strathfield.

In an interview shortly after the release of her novel *Whipping Boy*, the Australian writer Gabrielle Lord referred to her early 'hell' experience with the Dominicans at Strathfield.[2] According to Lord it was a brutal convent education. It has become fashionable for many literary works to exploit the theme of convent experience in Australia as one of psychotic incarceration. The topic certainly grabs a media audience.

Judy's account is somewhat different. For her teaching duties at Santa Sabina she was given junior secondary level and a little Year 11. She also had an extra free period once a week because she had to teach what for her was a totally new subject—French. 'I suppose they thought one foreigner could teach another a foreign language', laughs Judy. Like a lot of teachers thrown in to fill a space she was just one lesson ahead of the class.

Teaching is the art of the resourceful and Judy found that a Chinese girl from the New Hebrides was a valuable teaching aid. *There was a lovely little girl who spoke perfect French. She used to stand on the table for me and sing the French songs while the rest of us would learn them. She corrected my pronunciation, so that was lovely.*

Then there was Judy's English pronunciation. Her English was improving but when asked to teach it in Year 7 she was very embarrassed. How could she do justice to a subject she had barely begun to master? It would never happen in Hungary. Her request not to teach English was eventually granted and Judy took mathematics and geography or art and went on practising her English vowels so that she would one day be able to say 'How now brown cow whither goest thou?' just like any English lady.

Religious life in essence is an intense dimension of the spiritual life. Many fictional accounts and recollections of social history focus too readily on outward manifestations of daily practices and communal rubric. These depictions of disturbed starchily dressed nuns in dictatorial mode enforcing rules over every aspect of life, from writing letters to taking a bath, may make good stories and settings for television but the real struggle for the member of a religious community is inner conflict. By the fifth year of her Dominican life Judy was experiencing that inner struggle. It was aggravated by the demands of an excessive workload.

In the fifth year of my stay in the convent we were so

*busy. Young nuns were given an awful lot of jobs to do.
Cleaning the bathrooms, cleaning the common room
where we used to have recreation, taking up breakfast
and meals to old nuns, looking after the boarders,
cleaning different parts of the convent, preparing for
classes, corrections and of course the prayers. . . We were
not allowed to stay up until all hours of the night. We
went to bed at 10.30 with lights out and got up at 5.30.
And there were so many conflicts of not being able to
complete the tasks I was supposed to complete. It was very
frustrating.*

Judy was also studying pure mathematics by correspondence with the University of New England in Armidale. It
wasn't easy.

Two experiences that year were catalysts to break Judy's
contentment with her choice of religious life as the best
setting for her spiritual harmony. As was customary for the
correspondence students at Armidale, Judy and one other
member of her community studying pure mathematics were
required to attend a two-week live-in series of lectures.
Released from the busy schedule at Santa Sabina the two
young nuns could only enjoy themselves, listening to inten-
sive classes rather than piecing together difficult concepts
from printed notes. It was invigorating and it opened another
door for Judy.

A retreat in Maitland given by Father Peter Knowles, now
at Monash University, provided the second jolt.

*We had a wonderful retreat on the Christian life. Father
Knowles extolled the beauties of the Christian
experience—whether you are a religious or otherwise.
That was the final kick which helped me with my hidden
difficulty of being in the convent. I felt that my purpose
was to reach perfection through the religious life. But if it
wasn't leading me to perfection what was the point of it.
And if it was possible to reach it in some other form of
Christian life why should I keep on in a way that
hindered me.*

About six months before her vows were due to be
renewed Judy told her superiors that she wanted to leave.
There was no pressure for her to rethink. It was agreed that

she should stay to finish the teaching year then leave. And that is what she did, returning to Melbourne to take a job commencing in February at Fitzroy Girls Secondary School and to live once again with the Hughes family. It was 1964. The momentous years of change within Catholic religious communities around the world, set in chain by the Second Vatican Council in Rome, were beginning. Judy had escaped once again although this time unwittingly.

During her time in the Dominican order Judy had become an Australian, in 1963. She had been advised by the prioress of the convent to take out citizenship in case Australia became involved in a war. This was the era of the Cuban missile crisis and the height of Cold War politics between the USSR and the USA. Judy was from Communist Hungary and Australia was an ally of the United States. The prioress told Judy that in the event of a war Hungarians in Australia might be interned and this would mean Judy would have to leave the convent. Judy remembers at the time being more worried about having to leave the convent than being interned. However, as things turned out she left the convent as an Australian citizen.

At Fitzroy Girls School Judy found herself among another immigrant community—Greek girls coping with school in Australia. There was an immediate affinity. Their Hungarian refugee teacher took them over the rudiments of their new language in a subject called 'English as a Second Language'. She drew them diagrams and drawings and they had fun along the way. It was an experience she understood and that was an important help.

University beckoned. Armidale had made that a clear goal. For a year Judy studied applied mathematics at Melbourne University, at an evening course, hoping to save enough money to attend full time the following year. For those of us old enough to remember, there were fees to pay then as well as the cost of surviving without an income. Austudy and fee-less universities were more than a decade away. In addition Judy wanted a place at a residential college so as not to waste time travelling. Fervent as ever she had begun pursuing the next dream.

Mother Frances at St Mary's College, a residential college operated by the Loreto nuns, listened when approached and offered a reduced rate for a year. She was sympathetic to this older student who had spent some years in a convent and who was beginning her studies with so many handicaps. By the end of the year, with her salary from Fitzroy Girls and penurious living, Judy had saved enough to live sparingly at St Mary's and begin full time studies at Melbourne University, taking physics, chemistry and the history and philosophy of science. There was also the possibility of winning a mature age scholarship at the end of first year.

In recorded and unrecorded recollections of Melbourne University of the mid-1960s there are many accounts of the life of the embryonic artist posing as a newly released adolescent from some secondary college or other. The stories exaggerate and embellish the raffish undergraduate experience, focusing on endless examples of aberrant behaviour and the fresh feeling of independence. For all that the impression gained on reading these accounts is a womb-like atmosphere endangered only by hard work and the loss of a mummy or daddy in the shadows ready to pick up the tab. The accounts have in common the ring of a student golden age revisited. The reminiscences of Suzanne Ingleton (Miss University 1962) in *Memories of Melbourne University* convey something of undergraduate sensibilities around the time Judy became a Melbourne University fresher:

> The people in my year were extremely dull looking, unglam and reserved. The males wore short hair, thousands of pairs of spectacles and last year's grey school trousers and their fathers' ties. The women were definitely the skirt-and-cardy brigade with a few exceptions—mainly Me of course. Oh God, why is it my fate, I thought, doomed to five years' bonhomie with this lot? Whilst, there, one year above me, strolled some of the most divine looking individuals I'd ever seen. Not recognising the simple fact that this is what one year's exposure at Uni does to people . . .[3]

Twice removed from the Suzanne Ingleton view of university life by refugee and convent encounters, Judy remembers a glorious year at St Mary's fully enlivened by the ready availability of university studies. She had no money, she was five years older than others in her year, she had been separated from ordinary society in Melbourne after only a brief time as a school girl and her family was miles away in Hungary and Israel. She should have been nagged by doubts and a sense of being an outsider but she wasn't. One student who later became a friend remembers her at a Newman Society orientation camp. She was the odd one out, but perfectly happy, saying little and singing with noticeable gusto. While younger freshers like Miss Ingleton were competing to be Miss University, 'getting heavily into mascara' or challenging gender stereotypes like normal eighteen year olds, Judy was being turned on by the simplest of pleasures— just being there.

Hanging over Judy's head that year was the prospect of not getting the mature age scholarship that would finance her studies in second and third year. And that is exactly what happened. There was one term's money left for St Mary's but Mother Frances, with all the practical good sense of any landlady, thought using it would be unwise as Judy's room would have to be filled again after only one term. So Judy moved into a house with seven others in Carlton close to the university, made possible by a new phenomenon that had entered her financial arrangements. She had made just enough money to begin another year by working all summer making academic gowns.

I was so poor and money was so tightly budgeted that when I went to St Mary's and had to wear an academic gown I could not possibly buy one. So I took very accurate engineering measurements from one of the other gowns and went into Myers and bought one of the cheapest materials which would do the job and I made it. It took me about two to three days.

Desperate for income at the end of first year Judy realised that she could make money selling academic gowns to students at the residential colleges when university resumed. All she needed was a loan for the materials. Father Jerry Golden, the university chaplain, decided the idea was worth the risk and lent her £100. She bought rolls and rolls of black material from the Job Warehouse in Bourke Street and made 100 gowns. She stitched them on Mrs Hughes' treadle sewing machine, working all the summer holidays. Then she went along to the university colleges and sold them. Father Golden regained his £100 investment and Judy established her very own summer sweat shop that would bring her in extra cash each 'gown season' for the next fourteen summers.

It is a fashionable artistic self-indulgence to muse about impoverished student digs and smelly (rites of) passages of Joycean darkness. Suzanne Ingleton recalls the 'various threads of student life being lived out in various terraces, lofts and rat holes around the Uni'. In such musings there is little angst at lack of income and it is not uncommon to find that the worst that could happen to the inhabitants of these 'various . . . rat holes' is a forced reliance on a family allowance. For the student of an immigrant experience like Judy, however, without the security of a settled family, poverty is nothing to boast about and certainly not chic. It is seen as a trap and often forces the individual on beyond conventional avenues.

When Judy took a look at her bank balance after the gowns had been sold it became evident that she would need to work harder at a way to finance her year at university. Living in the little Carlton room had few attractions but it might not be possible to pay even that small rent without further income. She thought about the scholarship. *I went along to the Board which was the scholarship authority for Melbourne University and found out that I was two or three down the list from those who had got the mature age scholarship. If any of these dropped out I would get it. And in time I did get it.*

Suddenly there were no fees to pay and in time there was a small living allowance. To add to her success Judy found a position as a maid at Newman College. The job required waitressing at the tables in the evenings and helping with the cleaning of the dining room on Saturdays. Included with the position was a room at Newman College in a separate staff quarters. Judy chortles a line of Gilbert and Sullivan as she recalls how happy she was. At the end of that year she met Joe.

My ninety-minute tape has been turned over by this stage as Judy recounts her story. We are sitting in the living room of her Wattle Glen home. Youngest daughter Jenny has been out of bed for an hour or so after recovering from a late night. Joe asks if we would like some afternoon tea and we say yes please. Jenny is already making telephone calls planning her Saturday evening out. Her older sister Catherine is having the year off from work to travel and is in Paris. Second daughter Elizabeth lives with university friends in inner Melbourne. They are typical of many Australian families. And as a typical Australian family they are multicultural. Yet Judy also reflects a common mood of recessionary times and is troubled by the arguments that governments are sponsoring separate cultures. Closely questioned she is not sure what it all means, however. She admits to knowing very little about Vietnamese and Italian communities, like most Australians. Challenged she admits she is occasionally guilty of stereotyping. She is worried by ethnic gatherings one minute and expresses delight about watching Hungarian children performing national dances and speaking perfect English the next. In theory Judy is against 'multiculturalism', like much of middle Australia. Asked to think more deeply about it, she discovers she has become confused by a label. In fact she and her family are part of the multiculture dimension.

Talking to Judy about the issues of migration and settlement it is clear that her responses offer a warning to the politician who thinks there are votes in an anti-migrant stance. Polls suggest a majority of Australians do not favour immigration and think money is being wasted on helping immigrants. But while both Judy and Joe learnt English without government help, like Rita and Lily before them, Judy believes firmly that government money should be spent on helping migrants to learn English when they come to Australia. She is also not opposed to a generous intake of migrants even in a recession. Like many, her attitudes are formed by a mixture of personal experience and the political fashions of the day.

Looked at another way the ethnic group can be an important settling-in feature of any immigrant's life. It brings people together who, after struggling with a foreign language all day, can spend a few hours in company where they can once again speak naturally. Many of the Hungarian immigrants who came to Australia after 1956 were separated from their former families. In the group of singles where Judy met Joe there were only two women who were not divorcees. Judy was one of them. The group organised singles' parties. To attend a person had to be Hungarian, single and invited by a member of the group. *We got together at a different person's place each time. The ladies used to bring a plate of food and the gentlemen would take a bottle of drink. We would have the most wonderful civilised party—dancing, eating, drinking and in wonderful conversation.*

Keeping in touch with Australian Hungarians has been part of Judy's life since 1957 in spite of having no family with her. Father Fazokas, her mentor at St Dominics, lectured to a group at the Hungarian centre in Elgin Avenue, Armadale, a Melbourne suburb between Toorak and Caulfield, where Judy went to hear him give seminars on philosophy and theology. She also went there for dances and functions from her home in Kew not very far away. For a time the centre was the hub of Hungarian life. At the centre Judy met the man who years later would introduce her to Joe.

Hungarian-born Australian Andrew Riemer in his *Inside Outside: Life Between Two Worlds* accepts Australia, after considerable intellectual angst, as 'the only society with which I am at all familiar . . . where I feel least alien'. Yet he laments the lack of romantic culture in modern Australian society, looking back wistfully on a British culture that gave some succour to those 'powerful longings—romantic, idealistic, seeking for beauty . . . through books, through a version of history. . .'.[4] Driving along the Henry Lawson/Banjo Paterson rolling hills of the Greensborough Bypass and through Diamond Creek to Judy's house, listening to the Fureys, Davey Arthur and the Wolfe Tones singing Irish ballads on my hire car tape deck, this judgement seemed a bit skewed. Empire world traditions are not the whole of it. Perhaps Hungarian-born Riemer had been too focused on Anglophilia, I thought. There are other traditions that roam in the soul Down Under. For Judy Australia and its inspiration, romantic or otherwise, has never paled. Yet Judy, Hungarian like Riemer, empathised strongly with his autobiography and like Riemer she is apprehensive about losing the British tradition as an identity for Australia. *Economically we are pretty independent of Britain. But I think it is a very important connection and the Britishness of our tradition is important to me.*

For the first generation of immigrants the accumulation of

financial security for their children is a life long goal. Frugality, hard work and ingenious planning to exploit any opportunity are the focus of survival. The harshness of the immigrant experience and its raw new wave multiculturalism have brought an honesty and sharpness to the Australian vision. But for many like Judy Anglophile traditions are also important. For Judy this has meant a combination of things, such as the characteristic easy sense of humour and the freedom from the old divisions she remembers in Europe. In her early years in Australia she remembers an exchange with a woman at the Royal Melbourne Hospital about whether she was Hungarian or Jewish. Only then did she realise that in Australia there was no harm in admitting to either.

Married life for Judy and Joe has reflected a commonplace struggle up the crystal mountain to be found in Judy's painting of Saturn. They are typical of many Australians. By the time they were married they had established a valuable collection of friends, Hungarian and non-Hungarian. One of the special features of Australian life is the ready network of friendships that can be quickly made. From the day I met Judy we became close friends. My mother and my friends who came to know Judy and Joe quickly accepted them as part of the friendship network. In times of need, which weren't often, we stuck together.

Judy and Joe began married life in a small bedsit with rudimentary kitchen and bathroom in Church Street, Fitzroy. On visits Judy would educate me in intuitive Hungarian cooking, browning specially coated chicken or vegetables in her simple frying pan. I would wash up her choked kitchen bench of dirty dishes. During the summer holidays the room was filled with the black shapes of fabric, piled about the small room as the gowns were tacked together for the next academic season. For the years Judy sewed them they were assembled in unairconditioned rooms cramped with family furniture and belongings, and during two seasons Judy was pregnant. On Christmas Day in the first year of their marriage Judy and Joe became the parents of Catherine and that year Judy finished the last subjects for her degree.

In Hungary Joe had been a farmer. With more than a hundred acres of land he had been classified as a kulak and was imprisoned as a class enemy. In Australia he studied at night school and became a draughtsman, eventually beginning a long career with Alcan. A year after Catherine was born Judy and Joe bought their first home, choosing to live close to Joe's work in the northern suburbs at Broadmeadows. Practical considerations were paramount once again. Living close to work was essential when for years the family car was an ageing Ford Prefect.

The great Australian dream is now Judy's. And Joe has his hobby farm, complete with hazelnut orchard and vegetable patch. In European style Joe's rural expanse is laid out in sections. From the back terrace you can piece together the different plots: the dam with the water fowl, the paddock for Honey the mare, the hazelnut grove, the native trees about to make a small forest, the home garden near the house with fruit from raspberries to peaches and vegetables of every variety. After two careers, Judy as a teacher and Joe draughting for Alcan, they are subsisting on retirement benefits and stocked freezers of food from the land around them. For holidays they go to their beach house. The story of their crystal mountain is a familiar one—taking loans, sacking builders, buying and reselling, weekends doing home improvements. Australia's little home capitalists are all the same, whatever their ethnic origins.

In Australia Judy became friends again with her father when she began writing to him as a schoolgirl. Before she married she went back to Hungary visiting Joe's relatives for the first time. There have been many visits since and Judy's mother spent holidays in Australia before she died and was buried in Israel in 1991. Judy now has a sister in Israel and a brother in Belgium. Her daughters are discovering family ties in Europe for the first time, adding another layer to their Australian identity.

Judy has begun painting 'The Creation'. Her ethnic, biblical and scientific backgrounds are in sharp focus. She admits to an obsession that has been intensifying over twenty years. Through it she is discovering more and more about herself. But ask Judy what it means to be an Australian and the answer is cluttered with impressions. Then finally she says: 'I don't know whether I can define being an Australian'.

Lilah

MORE House in Tite Street, Chelsea, was given feature spreads in two of London's glossier home and interior magazines in January and February 1990. One of the articles noted:

> Counting the various Hope-Nicholson nephews and nieces who sporadically occupy its thirteen bedrooms, the house has been home to the same family for five generations: only Buckingham Palace can claim a longer pedigree for a London residence. But it is the Hope-Nicholsons themselves who make this particular corner of Chelsea's history extraordinarily alive.[1]

Both magazines offered luscious colour photos of select rooms to be found in More House. Modern photographic equipment complete with dazzling lighting and days of restorative cleaning had contributed to the stunning effects. Any visitor to More House in 1990 saw that the real thing was all the more endearing for being closer to a shut away, Miss Havisham setting, untouched by housekeeper or renovator. Its senior inhabitants, octogenarian Margaret Hope and her somewhat younger cousin and owner of the house, the late Felix Hope-Nicholson, lived lives of spartan frugality in their museum, surrounded by priceless and decaying treasures. Just a few doors up from More House is the former home of Oscar Wilde, whose wife was a cousin of Adrian Hope, Felix's grandfather. Adrian Hope became guardian of Oscar Wilde's children after Wilde's imprisonment.

In Margaret's bedroom the walls are sky blue and the ceiling gold. The room, including its canopy bed complete with lumpy, chest high antique mattress, is a replica of Cardinal Richelieu's bedroom. As such of course its picture was included in both articles on More House. To anyone familiar with Margaret's room it appeared remarkably trans-formed by light and polishing when presented by *The World of Interiors* and *Country Homes*. But for me the most remark-able feature was on the dressing table. It was a photograph in a plain metal frame (circa 1980) of an Australian Carmelite nun. It was Lilah, of course.

When I left Rita and Anna, running late and headed for an appointment at a Carmelite convent, I was going to see Lilah. For more than twenty years I have visited my friend in the enclosed community in Stevenson Street, Kew. Her broad Oxford accent has remained unchanged by her Australian surrounds and the peace of convent life seems to have preserved for me the face of Lilah as I knew her at thirty, independent, reasonably free of family ties and working as a physiotherapist.

Personal or family visits to Carmel are limited to appoint-ments at monthly intervals. Interns, or those fully enclosed like Lilah, do not go outside the walls of the convent unless for urgent or official business. Still, there was no objection to my request to record something of Lilah's story. Mid-after-noon I stepped over the thick border of the massive security gateway and pulled at a large wooden knob hanging on rope that rings the door bell. It makes a metallic clang reminiscent of school days. One clang and Sister Elizabeth was letting me in as always. In the upstairs parlour, with someone's burglar alarm going off in outside suburbia for our backdrop, Lilah and I explored the past, she sitting upright on a straight-backed chair, me lounging forward on the settee.

Raised in an environment that was cluttered with upper middle class English ritual, Lilah has always tried to shrug off its pretensions. Her Catholic background may contribute to this a little, deriving from the dissenter tradition of true English Catholicism. With the Irish immigrant influx into England, in recent decades Catholics have become the largest single Christian group in England. But Lilah's family, on the fringes of the aristocracy, are of a different ilk. Their Catholicism, handed down for centuries by dissident English Catholics, is intellectual and has the fervour of belief held against the mainstream.

Genuine emancipation for English Catholics came only in the 1820s. After the 1830s the Oxford Movement led by John Henry Newman, a high Anglican, focused attention on the theological divisions between Anglicanism and Catholicism. For a time this threatened the unity of the Church of England. As Catholicism gained a precarious new foothold, the Vatican moved in 1850 to create English dioceses and made the conservative Cardinal Wiseman the first (post-Reformation) English Archbishop. On Guy Fawkes Day in the same year groups of English protestors burned effigies of the Pope and Wiseman. Unwittingly, in more recent times, English Catholicism with its intense conservatism has entertained millions through Evelyn Waugh's *Brideshead Revisited*. It was this tradition that inspired the Hopes to name More House after one of the great martyrs of English history, Thomas More. And Lilah herself explains the difference between English and Australian Catholicism in similar terms: 'There is less prejudice in Australia. It's never had the persecutions that England has had'. Lilah is Margaret Hope's niece.

I never knew Lilah in her English setting so I asked her why she had turned her back on the safety of nice English family connections. She replied without apology. *It's very fixed in England. I see the point of some of it now but in those days I couldn't at all. I rebelled against it a lot. It gives a graciousness to life but you know if you were of a certain class there was no social freedom.*

Lilah's grandfather was another who felt the pull of freedom away from England. Suffering from an asthmatic condition he went all the way to South Africa as a young man to settle. While the Hopes of Tite Street were mixing with Augustus John and John Singer Sargent, Lilah's grandfather was establishing a dynasty of Hopes emanating from Durban. *My grandfather was the only one of the Hopes who went to South Africa. So all the Hopes in South Africa are descended from him. The others are in Edinburgh mostly. Nearly all of my first cousins are still in South Africa. They have not thought of leaving. They just pray there will be no civil war.*

Lilah's mother, Patricia, and her Aunt Margaret were born and grew up in South Africa. Lilah's father was English. Her parents met aboard a ship on its way to South Africa when Lilah's mother was still only a schoolgirl. Lilah's father was the captain of the ship. Family folklore has it that in conversation the schoolgirl and the captain discovered they would each like a daughter one day so they could name her Anne. Years later they did. She was Lilah's older sister.

World War II made Lilah a South African. Her father was an Englishman based in England, but when the war made England unsafe Lilah's mother and sister evacuated to grandfather's property at Mooririvier 100 miles north-west of Durban, prosperous country near the Drakensberg. Lilah was born in Durban soon after. Her recollections of South Africa are sketchy as she was only a very small child when she lived there. *We had two acres, a cow, unmade roads and mass once a month. A neighbour kept some oxen to drag the cars out of the mud. It was because of my maternal grandfather's asthma that the family had settled there. South Africa was my first country and nationality as it was my land of birth.*

Lilah's earliest childhood was spent in a setting witnessing the last years of British colonial South Africa before the Boer governments after World War II ushered in a policy of apartheid. In Lilah's day black Zulu natives worshipped in the same congregations as white settlers. Their priests came from the French order of Oblates and the Sunday masses, in Latin, took place in the Catholic church near the Mooririvier sale yards.

The area, 5000 feet above sea level with its bald hills stripped of timber for the mines up on the Rand, is rich grazing country of pink-brown sourveldt grasslands. Further

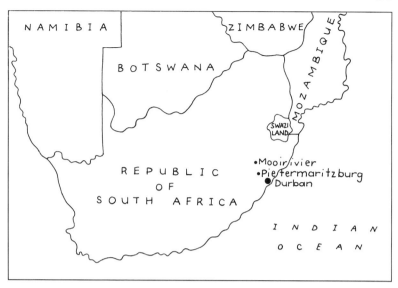

north is the sweetveldt. In the grasslands districts settlements of English and Scots, with plentiful supplies of cheap black labour, built up cattle and sheep runs and mixed farms. In return for the plots of land the white farmers gave their Zulu families, the children and some of the women would do the menial labouring tasks like weeding between the rows of crops. The men provided paid labour for the heavier farm jobs. This was the Africa of Karen Blixen.

It was also the Africa that worried Australia's Henry Gullett, head of the Bureau of Immigration, in 1920. Gullett recognised the attractions of Africa for 'the young Englishman of a good class'. In *Unguarded Australia* he expressed his concern that Australia could not attract such immigrants because it lacked excitement and cheap labour, saying, '. . .most young men with means and opportunity prefer life in countries in which money-making may be broken by occasional adventure'.[2] In South Africa there was plenty of opportunity to play the game hunter or local Livingston. However, British settlers also tended to reject the narrow attitudes of the Boers. One of Lilah's friends from the area, Peta York, now lives in Australia. She speaks with disdain of the name Pietermaritzburg, the district's capital, a name made up by combining the names of two prominent and, for Peta, detestable Boer leaders.

In 1940 the area around Mooririvier was still enjoying a

period of high colonialism. Settlers of English and Scottish descent had created a district of select society. Polo during winter months brought the families together each Saturday. The ladies took turns to prepare sumptuous teas and the play off for the final match coincided with the annual agricultural show in Pietermaritzburg at the end of the season. Johnny Gibson, father of South Africa's great polo player Ian Gibson, taught Anne and Peta to ride at his riding school. Later, as a tiny tot, Lilah joined them. Peta can still remember the big black Wolseley Lilah's mother drove them in, the first car in the area.

In 1946, the earliest they could get a passage, Lilah's mother took her daughters back to join their father in England. They went to live at Boars Hill outside Oxford. The English climate left Lilah sickly for a lot of her childhood. When she was thirteen her father died.

As a girl Lilah attended Sacre Coeur, Roehampton, which had moved to Waldingham after the war. Vivien Leigh is listed among its more famous old girls. Lilah then trained in physiotherapy at St Thomas Hospital which involved moving to London and flatting in the usual style with friends. But by the time she was 24 Lilah had booked her passage for Australia under the assisted passage agreement with England.

For an Australian, Lilah's education and her career as a physiotherapist would seem to fit well with her privileged middle class background and be unlikely to direct her towards an immigrant life. However, as a young woman Lilah began to question the security of her social position. She now considers this was due to her London experience.

To begin with it was unusual I think for someone of my social status at that time, but not now, to train as a physio. And in training you met far more of a cross-section of society than anyone of my home background would ever meet normally, particularly in the hospitals I worked and trained in. I trained and worked on the edges of the slums which my class never came in contact with. I suppose that probably set me thinking. These decisions are never taken lightly or quickly. I had some Australian friends, two in particular worked for Australia House. They told me about the assisted passage. At the same time I had far too many female relatives trying to run my life for me. As one South African female relative once said, 'I am not surprised you are going to Australia'. That also had something to do with it.

Moreover, Lilah's family in England was thinning out. Anne had married a lawyer and they had moved to Vancouver. Lilah's mother was already thinking of selling up the family home in Boars Hill and joining her elder daughter in Canada. She had never been entirely happy in England. After careful consideration then, in 1964, Lilah accepted an assisted passage flight to Australia.

At various periods in Australian history the single British woman has been attracted by life Down Under. In the nineteenth century Caroline Chisholm worked tirelessly to settle hundreds of young and often destitute British women, who mostly became wives of settlers in a colony overpopulated by men. By the turn of the century emigration schemes were once more targeting single British women. Geoffrey Sherington in *Australia's Immigrants* draws attention to the increasing numbers of upwardly socially mobile young British women coming to Australia in the years before World War I.[3] The young women were encouraged to continue the civilising mission of English womanhood begun by the women of the nineteenth century. By the time Lilah emigrated such ingenuous campaigns were hardly necessary.

When Lilah arrived in Australia British immigration was at a peak. It was also a time when, with modern air travel, many British immigrants also returned home after finding it was not so far away any more. In the 1960s about a quarter of British migrants to Australia went back, although some of these returned. By the 1980s, however, the number of immigrants from the United Kingdom was on the decline and by 1987 it was only half of the size of the intake from Asia.

The idea of being able to purchase a ten pound ticket to life Down Under seems somewhat unbelievable in 1992. The scheme, however, lasted until 1981. Once in Australia Lilah's new found independence was guaranteed not only by the social freedoms of the 1960s but also by her comfortable financial circumstances. She had a small inheritance, accumulated from three or four uncles and aunts, and that private income made a lot of difference. She also had no difficulty finding a job and the task was made a lot easier by the fact

that she was English. *I got a job straight away. It was easy
to get work. Nowadays one has to go to the country practi-
cally. It is difficult. But certainly not then. Moreover I had
my English training and English experience after that training. That also made it easy.*

Immigrants with English-speaking backgrounds were def-
initely advantaged as newcomers. In the period Lilah came
to Australia, around 60 per cent of the qualifications of
migrants from English-speaking countries were accepted
while only 40 per cent of qualifications were accepted for
those from non-English-speaking countries. To Lilah and
many others her London training from St Thomas Hospital
was undisputedly superior. But looking back Lilah has reas-
sessed her views of Australian physiotherapists. *When I left
London it was a city of twelve million, the population of the
whole of Australia. In those days I felt the Australian training
in my profession was behind the English. That is why I got
overcritical. But not now. I think in fact these days Australia
is leading England in physiotherapy.*

It was not unreasonable that having chosen to settle in
Australia Lilah would still instinctively feel that the larger and
older civilisation led the way. That was only natural. And
Lilah's family anecdotes contained more than the usual connections with Australia. First there was the (not too) distant
cousin, John Hope. To Australians he is better known as Lord
Hopetoun. When Margaret Hope's brother Adrian was a small
boy his uncle, Adrian Hope, told him that by the time he was
thirty he would most probably have succeeded to the title.
But titles are very competitive and when new cousins were
born young Adrian missed out. John Hope, or Lord
Hopetoun, was Governor of Victoria between 1889 and 1895
and later returned to become Australia's first Governor-General. In Victoria he was an able head of state but his term as
Governor-General is chiefly remembered for the 'Hopetoun
Blunder' when he invited the Premier of New South Wales,
Sir William Lyne, to form the first Australian ministry. Sir
William was little known outside New South Wales and he
had consistently opposed federation. When Lyne could not
get the support he needed to form a ministry Hopetoun called
the much favoured Edmund Barton.

Then there was Dr Eric D'Arcy, a Catholic priest who was

a lecturer in philosophy at Melbourne University when Lilah arrived in Australia. He later became Archbishop of Tasmania. In Oxford Eric D'Arcy had been a visitor to Lilah's family home on a number of occasions. He had been studying for his DPhil, the first Australian-born graduate at Oxford to take a doctorate in philosophy. When deciding where to settle Lilah remembered Father D'Arcy and conversations about his university beat in the inner Melbourne suburb of Parkville and that helped her decide. She also knew one other family in Melbourne.

That is why I came to Melbourne. Eric D'Arcy, now His Grace, and one other family I knew of, which made a difference. Father D'Arcy recognised me in fact and claimed friendship with my family. The family in Melbourne I knew had a daughter who was leaving and I took her place in the flat. I made a friend, Georgina, and we shared the flat. It was in Parkville which made a tremendous difference. An ideal place to settle in when you come to Australia, full of people floating in that university atmosphere. A very ideal place to start. An outsider can fit in very quickly.

Lilah had indeed landed in a rarefied environment. Parkville, one of Melbourne University's dormitory areas, contained and still contains all the ingredients that would suit a daughter of middle class (albeit Catholic) English parents. Its boundaries are the university avenue of Royal Parade turning sharply into Gatehouse Street which flows into Flemington Road which completes the triangle that is Parkville proper. The area hasn't changed much since 1890, fronting on to tree-lined Royal Parade that borders the historic halls of residence on the other side—Janet Clarke Hall, Trinity College and the edges of Ormond College. Most of its terraces are renovated, these days in carefully authentic period colours, although some have lost a little grace as rooming establishments and occasional lots have given way to 'modern' 1950s, or thereabouts, apartment blocks. But on the whole the area is gentrified albeit understated in the tradition of London's Bloomsbury.

At St Carthage's in Royal Parade, the Parkville Catholic church, Lilah found another social milieu that suited her.

Gatherings, over soup and salad after mass on Sundays, with Paul and Aileen Grundy opened up a new and lively set of contacts. This semi-open house followed on from the late morning mass and as such brought together a loose collection of parishioner types who frequented St Carthage's. Aileen recalls not knowing some who came. Regulars included John and Christine Fox, the 'Terry Blakes', Aileen McLaughlin and former Jesuit scholastics like John Wolfensberger and John Leonard. One of the young Grundys used to talk of 'fox, wolf and leopard' coming to lunch. These open house get-togethers attracted mostly university graduates and academics, some married, some taking higher degrees and others drifting about as young professionals, drawn together by emerging intellectual freedom and theological discussion, in a church experiencing radical change. But equally most were not the radicals of the street march or demonstration.

Parkville was a fairly tolerant place for a new chum. Lilah remembers it fondly.

Parkville made a tremendous difference. I have always loved Australia although I think when one gets uprooted one tends to be critical for no reason. That is just because you're dumped in new surroundings. Still, I had a lot more back-up than many new migrants. I was very lucky being with a group of Catholics and that helped. Elsewhere it was not so easy. I was ticked off for the way I pronounced a name.

Her broad Oxford accent in fact often made Lilah sound foreign. Many thought her pronunciation was European. This was certainly the case when she registered to vote. *In those days British subjects had to register to vote within six months. I went along to the Post Office and they said that I should be naturalised first. They could not understand my accent.* Within a few years Lilah did become naturalised. She joined a minority of British immigrants to Australia who have chosen to surrender their British passports. *All you had to do in those days was to fill in a form. They checked the details and you received your certificate in the mail. I did not have to take the oath swearing allegiance to the Queen. It is different now. Even British immigrants have to swear allegiance.*

In 1966 Lilah moved out of Parkville to the racier cosmopolitan North Carlton. Property values were cheaper here and
Lilah was able to find a bargain cottage in Rathdowne Street,
a wide (then treeless) expanse of road stretching from the
Exhibition Gardens on the fringes of the central business
district to Park Street, Carlton's boundary with plebeian
Brunswick. The house with its fifteen foot frontage was just
the width of a footpath away from a bus stop. Its strip of
backyard was as long as the house again and had a right of
way to the remnants of a garage shelter from a small lane
coming in behind the houses next door. Even so Lilah opted
for parking her car on the other side of Rathdowne Street,
ready to make a series of left hand turns around the Carlton
cemetery to avoid right hand turns when she went visiting
in Parkville.

Acquiring a property was an important move. It made
Lilah independent, gave her a new status as a local and
somewhere to belong in a new environment. Having a small
plot of ground made her new surroundings more acceptable
as home. Yet Lilah was able to do this only because of ready
cash. In 1966 women were not able to borrow money for
mortgages and very few Australian women could afford cash
for a house of their own.

Lilah and I met by chance and have managed long years
of friendship in different phases as I moved from state to
state and she remained with the Carmelites. However, our
compatibility remains a mystery considering our very different backgrounds and temperaments.

When my final year of school was extended by another
twelve months so I could accumulate the required age to
enter university, I spent a year organising teams for sports
days, studying a few more subjects and staying very much
in the schoolgirl mould. At Melbourne University in 1967 I
began living away from home. When my first lodging
arrangement proved unsatisfactory I was told about Lilah
through a connection with the Grundys. After the usual
phone calls and checking, Lilah and I struck an accommodation arrangement and it lasted until I left university. In fact
Lilah moved on first when she joined the Carmelites.

Anti-multiculturalists are fond of playing up differences
which they believe must be overcome if those of native

English-speaking background are to co-exist with those of 'foreign' origins where English is not spoken. What these social engineers seem to ignore are the obvious cultural differences within the English-speaking world. Lilah was not only ten years my senior, she was set in ways that were in sharp contrast with mine. Yet we co-existed perfectly.

Perhaps a strict convent education helped, but when my young and casual Australian lifestyle met Lilah's formal English tradition it fell into line with uncharacteristic meekness. We had rules, laid down from the outset and explained to me as emanating from Lilah's experience of flatmates in London. And I agreed to everything. In fact the terms were easy. The rent was generously cheap and we lived just above the poverty line on a Lilah budget of ten dollars a week for food and groceries. One of our evening meals each week consisted of a bowl of soup followed by a rasher of bacon on one (unbuttered) slice of toast. We had cocoa and one biscuit each for supper. Housework and cleaning were shared. Lilah cooked, I washed up. In deference to scrupulous safety precautions, on cold winter evenings Lilah would pour a saucepan of water over the glowing mallee root in the open fireplace. It also meant the mallee root lasted another day.

In Rathdowne Street my ancient grey Ford Prefect (Bertha), parked facing south, signalled I was at home just as Lilah's new white VW Beetle (Lady Jane), parked facing north on the far side, signalled she was in residence. In time I acquired an Australian terrier and Lilah a cat. We shared the tiny two bedroom house, with outside bathroom and loo, equally. In everything but personal indulgence Lilah was very generous. But her wartime and English life had made her obsessively frugal. Thus I crossed a cultural void, learning to save hot water, to eat at meal times and not between, to save matches, string, paper and other useful materials, and to light a fire without kindling.

As the years passed a little extravagance crept in too. Lilah changed under the influence of her Australian milieu though never to the extent of sounding less English or, in spite of a healthy and ironic sense of humour, throwing off a somewhat formal drawing room demeanour. We acquired a rented television set, a set of bookshelves and, eventually, a passably nice garden. After one or two summers Lilah actually appeared to have a slight suntan and was taking on a healthier Australian appearance.

Lilah's move to North Carlton meant that she shed the hothouse university atmosphere of Parkville and placed herself in an area where migrant and local working class people shared space with the cash-strapped rooming student. In the late 1960s the Melbourne University's student housing service still found very affordable accommodation for students in the many yet-to-become-fashionable terraces and semis littering the suburb. This was in spite of massive 'slum' clearance (many said the best houses were demolished) and the erection of monolithic blocks of Housing Commission flats at the southern end of Rathdowne Street and Lygon Street. In some cases old rent-control legislation still applied keeping down rents, supposedly to help the poor. In the new St Mary's College magazine for 1966 Libby Redmond, tongue firmly in cheek, summed up the difference between Parkville and Carlton:

> By the grace of God and the Melbourne City Council, St Mary's College is in Parkville—ten feet away from social ignominy. Had our post box been on the other side of Swanston St., our letters would have been stamped CARL-TON—a name which leads to involuntary thoughts of derelict houses, the cemetery, dingy rooms, cabbages, the brewery and those monstrous flats.

Carlton and its slightly more respectable northern extension could certainly be described as a mixed bag. Greek and Italian grocery businesses offered cheap and convenient after hours service, along with the beginnings of some ethnic choice in foodstuffs. The very Australian newsagent a few doors from Lilah's house, however, had sons being educated by the Jesuits. For a while one caught sight of radical student leader Pete Steedman's Porsche parked outside a Carlton address in the days when he was in the forefront of the protest movement against capitalism, its works and its pomps. Meanwhile, at the city baths opposite the Rathdowne Street flats, migrant and inner city kids screamed away the summers while the bitumen pavements and playgrounds went soft in the near century heat.

The flavour of Carlton was captured in 1968 by the cameras of *National U*, the national university newspaper. On page 3 it reproduced a photo of university law student Heather Webb in provocative pose, arm around a human-sized fire hydrant. She was clad in the fashions of the day—long white leather boots and thigh-length shift dress. The headline was *She'll do 'U'*. The short write-up declared her to be 'kinda cute' and made suggestions of a phallic nature about Heather's effect against the hydrant. Readers were asked to 'check the baby photo' if in doubt. Then the piece continued with: 'Normally Heather is a second-year student at Melbourne University, as well as an almost emancipated member of the Liberal Club (ie she's about to join the Labor Club), who likes leather jackets and boots (but owns suede), motor-cycles (but can't ride), and booze (but can't hold it). She's a 'U' staffer.'

In 1968 it was very 'U' to be sexist in a good cause. Meanwhile, Heather's Carlton backdrop displayed a paling fence, edged with long stringy weeds, and a cracked pavement. 'Non-U' and very 'U' together. That was Carlton.

It was an age when the university environs were an extension of an elite subculture in the golden days of the university, a naive and blinkered period when Vice Chancellors posed confidently for Orientation Week magazines holding high, at the tips of fingers, the compulsory filtertip cigarette. It was an age when academic opinion was always regarded as expert and biology professors were asked their opinions on Communism and American involvement in Vietnam merely because they were academics. It was also an era when the radical student literature exploited women's bodies in a way that makes the much protested 1990s advertising industry look puritan. Many of these 1960s models went on to become vigorous feminists. And it was a time when student activists dominated the campuses. In 1968 *The Sydney Morning Herald* cartoonist Molnar depicted a student leader addressing a following with the words, 'We German students riot to support the Swedish students who riot to support the English students who riot to support the French students who riot to support us'.

In those days, and ever since, I seem to have befriended an unfashionable lot. At Melbourne University I had begun these associations by helping Gerard Henderson advertise lunchtime meetings, until having chalked the name 'Knopfelmacher' so many times on the pavements at night I could spell it without the help of notes. Frank Knopfelmacher (Franta), a lecturer in psychology at Melbourne University and an émigré from Czechoslovakia, was an opponent of totalitarianism, a term not widely used at the time. As such he opposed the activities of the left on campus whose protest demonstrations usually supported the totalitarian Ho Chi Minh, Communist ruler of North Vietnam.

At Lilah's we put together the Gestetner stencils for Gerard's anti-left newsletter *Public*. In the 1960s all student newsletters had that Gestetner look, some with staples at the margins. No doubt to Lilah it all had the hum of the ardent and the young. However Lilah also understood our unfashionable position. Her intellectual grounding in English Catholicism made her sceptical of slogan-chanting demonstrators and she did not regard us as lepers in the way others did. Equally, at the Grundys on Sunday mornings, she was perfectly at home with the other side of politics. John Fox was busy writing for *The Catholic Worker* sponsoring the causes of the left.

As a homeowner Lilah became very settled surprisingly quickly. But her interest in her surrounds remained very English. In *The Immigrants*, the English woman Alwine recalls an experience on a village bus in England some years after she had been living in Australia. When an elderly lady fell over, the bus stopped, the passengers all concerned themselves with the lady's needs and waited for an ambulance to arrive without grumbling about the delay. Alwine realised, as she sat watching, that instinctively she had removed herself from the scene and that inwardly she was impatient at the fuss. On reflection she was suddenly shocked to find she had become Australian, in that she was 'taking no notice'.[4]

Australia's sprawling suburbs have often been accused of alienating their inhabitants from one another. Certainly there are neighbourhoods where local contact is at a minimum. In Carlton with its diverse cultures and itinerant student intake it was easy to take no notice. I certainly came and went in the Australian way, using what I needed and leaving no trace.

Lilah on the other hand was much more in the village mould. Shopkeepers, librarians, bank tellers, tradesmen were all part of Lilah's local scene. She kept in friendly contact with them as she borrowed books, purchased the week's small hoard of food, deposited money or made home maintenance calls. Occasionally it was repaid in kind, with a few dollars off the bill when something needed mending.

When Lilah moved to Australia she brought very little, of course, furnishing her house in good buys and cheap secondhand pieces and keeping to her budget. A year or so after I moved in Lilah took delivery of some large crates that had been sent to her from London. They contained a number of things from home and for a few days Lilah was brought back into contact with familiar faces, shapes and feelings as she unpacked them. The crates sat in the narrow hall like giant invaders, giving up their armoury of treasures almost reluctantly as we talked about where to put them all. There were thirty large white dinner plates with scalloped edges. Each was marked with the fleur-de-lis of the family crest. There was a lot of silver cutlery which was unceremoniously stored in the cheap kitchen drawer under the sink. There were paintings, one by an early French Impressionist and another from the school of Van Dyck; there were books, some ancient and leather-bound, one a seventeenth century Ben Jonson. There were Peter Rabbit books from the 1940s and other children's literature, family photographs, trinkets and mementos aplenty. The collection took weeks to sort out. For Lilah it was all pleasure. There were no bookshelves for some time so the books were stacked in piles along the sitting room wall. When the draughts in winter crept in under the door that let out to the side path that led into the yard, Lilah would choose from among the piles some of the best volumes to block the gap at the floor. The Ben Jonson and a hefty nineteenth century bible were favourites.

As if out of the pages of a Barbara Pym novel visitors came to Rathdowne Street from time to time. There were hardly any who overstayed their welcome but those not accustomed to the house rituals could always be reminded of the late hour when Lilah emerged from her 'ablutions', in dressing gown and slippers, to wind the clock and put the cat out. When this happened my 'younger' guests would have to talk very quietly or move on. Among those who occasionally stayed the night was Lilah's friend Anne Clarke, postgraduating somewhere and no longer at St Mary's. Anne had rules of her own, which we carefully tried to observe, such as not being able to respond to conversation until she had been awake an hour or two. Among other visitors of note there was Eric D'Arcy.

Father D'Arcy seemed large in the same way Lilah's house was small. He came to dinner a couple of times and I joined in. Days before, Lilah worked out her menu and starched her voluminous linen table napkins that had arrived with the crates. Invariably the starch would bring the napkins to board-like stiffness and with ironing they folded into lap-sized squares easily mistaken for a new style of table mat. At dinner it took seconds to calculate that the napkin was not for turning. Except for Eric D'Arcy. With all the authority invested in him he could break open the starched napkin in just under a minute and a half, and conversation barely lagged as he did it. With aplomb he placed the crinkled white board on his knee and moved on to survey the meal.

That is all twenty years ago and more now. Before long Eric D'Arcy was a prelate of the church and far removed from taking dinner in small neighbourly kitchens. Although his ministry has coincided with quieter times for clerical administrators, there have been tussles nonetheless. In 1992 Archbishop D'Arcy closed St Mary's College in Hobart to cries of outrage and dismay from parents and local interest groups. A 'Save St Mary's' campaign was launched. Looking through the reports I couldn't help thinking of Eric D'Arcy in Lilah's kitchen. I noted that his administrative approach had all the hallmarks of his assault on one of Lilah's starched English napkins. And it was not good news for the parents in the Save St Mary's campaign.

My last year with Lilah straddled the end of my degree and the beginning of the hands-on study attached to a Diploma of Education. It also straddled her decision to enter Carmel and her mother's visit. Lilah had been to Vancouver to holiday with her family and now it was time for her mother to make her first trip to Australia. With no relatives in Australia Lilah, as a Carmelite, would not see her family again unless they visited her in Melbourne. *The step of entering*

*took about a year, because of various circumstances on both
sides. My mother coming over to live for a while was good
for me at that time. I was able to tell her about Carmel, face
to face, before I entered. And she was able to see Australia
which was quite something.*

Planning for Mama's visit took time. The tiny house had
been given some fundamental renovations when Lilah took
possession. The boards had been stained, some walls painted
white, a good hot water system had been installed and there
was some carpet in the sitting room. To put Mama up for a
month to six weeks would mean vacating a room. It was
decided I would move in with Di Martin's rooming establish-
ment in Royal Parade, Parkville, Lilah would renovate her
room for Mama and take my room for the visit. And we would
meet Mama in Adelaide, off the train from Perth after a sea
voyage via South Africa, and drive slowly back to Melbourne
showing her something of Victoria and South Australia on
the way. We prepared for the occasion like a city getting
ready for royalty. Even the garden took shape after years of
neglect. On one memorable Saturday morning we enlisted
some help to remove the furniture from Lilah's bedroom so
it could be painted. The furniture and contents which had
been part of the room only for four years resisted the move
with all the obstinacy of a lifetime's occupancy. Australia
could change some personality traits at the margin but Lilah's
English tendency to gather and amass small personal collec-
tions had remained intact.

Sometimes Lilah brings one of the convent's Great Danes
with her when I visit. There is always the shock of watching
such a large amount of canine come into the room but the
dogs, which are in Lilah's charge, are always impeccably
disciplined. Talking to Lilah in the convent parlour is a
relaxed affair in a formal surround lightly furnished with
donations of parlour lounge suite, piano, pictures, coffee
table and so on. The polished boards in a clear gloss and
the rugs scattered sparingly are spruce and free of any speck
of dust. There is no trace of chaos as on the morning when
we shifted the odd assortment of furniture from the
Rathdowne Street bedroom. That day itself marked something
of a watershed for Lilah. She never really returned to the
settled, snug tucked-away world of the small house and its

contents. Mama's visit brushed away the last cobweb. The time passed successfully and Mama proved to be a robust gardener and energetic socialiser. Lilah added another dimension to her life in Melbourne—a family. Mama made friends with Lilah's friends and the gap for Lilah between being a newcomer and being part of her adopted culture reduced a bit more.

Meanwhile I was experiencing the delight of being able to amble, minutes before class, across Royal Parade to the university from Number 99. Having spent the first night in Richard Thwaites' bed (he was away at the time), I moved on to occupy Di Martin's sitting room on a foldaway mattress. Di made a little extra profit from the rent for the time I was there. On afternoons when there was occasion to be in it was not unusual to meet Dennis Pryor, lecturer in Classics, coming to visit. At Number 99, academic pretensions thickened the atmosphere. Australian Rules football was regarded as some kind of foreign devil; most feigned ignorance of its existence. People were on guard not to make unlettered slips. By the time Mama went back to Canada I was a little relieved to be rejoining Lilah in her 'English' patch in egalitarian Carlton.

The world at large in 1970 offered the usual contradictions of human endeavour. When Lilah stepped over the line between world and monastery walls Charles Manson had not yet been convicted for the murder of Hollywood's Sharon Tate, white Mr Ian Smith headed the government of Rhodesia, a country with a black majority, and Gough Whitlam 'believed' he would be the next Prime Minister. Mr Whitlam was only half right. He would win the 1972 election but he was not to be the *next* Prime Minister. Billy and Sonia McMahon would inhabit the Lodge for a brief time before Gough and Margaret Whitlam arrived. At the University of California Issacs Bonewits, aged twenty, had just received the first degree in magic; Peter Yarrow of 'Peter, Paul and Mary' would shortly receive a sentence of three months jail on charges of taking 'indecent liberties' with a fourteen year old girl; US Vice-President Spiro Agnew had agreed to the sale of Mickey Mouse watches with his own cartoon on the dial; and in Britain divorce laws were about to be softened allowing divorce on the grounds of adultery only, provided it was proven that the adulterer was 'intolerable' to live with. In 1970 one in three rich people lived in New South Wales but Victoria was not far behind, while Queensland could manage only one rich person in eight. At the end of the year Barry Humphries was given a twelve month literary grant of $6000 to help him live while writing a play and a novel. Which were they I wonder?

By the time Lilah joined the Carmelites she knew what she was undertaking. She had spent months talking her decision over with the Mother Prioress at different interviews, had read widely from selected literature and had considered the step she was taking very carefully. *I suppose I've always known about Carmel. I've had a great devotion to Saint Teresa of Avila. I did not choose an active life in another order because I think I was shown the power of prayer. You can do wonderful good works, but prayer can go out to thousands throughout the world.*

The Order of Mount Carmel, as it's officially called, was restored to an austere and contemplative character in 1562 by Teresa of Avila. Today it is the largest contemplative order in the world. The Rule of the order is still read once each week in the refectory, couched in the language of sixteenth century Spain, referring to the need to 'beg when travelling' and allowing 'if necessary the keeping of asses and mules'. But adaptation and modification have crept in. Life is still strictly enclosed but there is more contact now with the outside world than at any time in the order's history. The floor to ceiling iron grille that separated the community from those on the other side is long gone. And the nuns all keep up with daily news reports.

The Midrash, a collection of Jewish commentaries on the scriptures, tells us: 'All beginnings are difficult'. After one year as a postulant, novices entering religious life have an initial two years while they continue to adapt to community life and master the detail of the Divine Office, said daily. In a Carmelite convent there are five hours of community prayer each day and two hours of personal prayer. Each undertaking involves careful adjustment. Lilah's novice mistress was Sister Patricia, who explains the process as one of guided spirituality.

The role of the novice mistress is to be a guide. In our

*life, every person has an individual way to find God.
There is a broad overall Carmelite spirituality, but within
that pattern everyone is called to an eternal life. The
Holy Spirit, the novice mistress or whoever must be a
guide. But they must be careful that they don't interfere
or direct as they think the person should be. So the
novice mistress must ask questions and encourage the
novice to talk. You ask them how they join in the prayer
because two hours of personal prayer is difficult at first.
The novices naturally have to go through the dramas of
faith and they need guidance as to how they can
approach God. And the guidance from experience and
past teachers is there for them. Just being in community
is also a great help for them. We are all together at
recreation, meals, saying the Divine Office so they pick it
up. But time is also given.*

When Lilah joined the Carmelites Divine Office was said
entirely in Latin. At first Lilah had Latin lessons to help. Saying
the Office requires each nun to take her turn chanting or
singing parts alone before the whole community. At Com-
pline or Matins or Vespers there are psalms, sacred verse,
tunes and harmonies all laid down for daily prayer by the
Bishops of Australia. Today the Office is said in English and
Lilah sees this as much better, especially as it is now possible
to rearrange and adapt the music within the convent itself.
Yet it was not the routines that Lilah found most difficult.

*Well I think my trouble was that I was not flexible
enough. Routine's fine; you just get out the program, set
yourself off on automatic pilot and away. But learning
flexibility is a surprising aspect of Carmel. Here it's all
very well thinking you can do A, B, C, D and E during
the day—then someone comes along and asks you to do
something totally different and that's what you do. I
learnt flexibility here. They say that self-will dies half an
hour after you are dead. I mean we all have it.*

Since Lilah entered other changes have affected the way
of life in the Melbourne Carmelites. There is now a 'Desert
Carmel', an hour or so away from Kew, in view of the sea
and small, relaxed and solitary. Here all the sisters spend
some time at various intervals. They keep up the Divine

Office while staying at Desert Carmel but the rubric is more staggered and personal. Monastic life is sustained but refreshed. There is no compulsion to go to Desert Carmel. In monastic life, Sister Patricia explains, a member of the community can request a move to another convent but she cannot be told she has to go. Since joining the Carmelites Lilah has also seen much more of her family than she expected to when she entered. And her mother alone has made numerous visits to Melbourne, staying in the convent in a special flat set aside for visitors.

There have been no difficulties being so far from my family. My mother's family has a history of living in different countries and once that's in the background I have noticed that one learns to cope. Sometimes my non-Australian origins have caused slight misunderstandings—a look or something said with a different nuance—but that is no different from anywhere. There were certainly moments when I wanted to leave. But I came here with the intention that I was going to stay and knew that to leave fundamentally would be the wrong decision. Sometimes you react suddenly to situations, I think one does in marriage too, but you know it would be wrong. Being a nun doesn't mean you stop being a human being.

Taken as a whole the Catholic Church is the great multi-cultural institution of the world. Its fabric is woven in more languages and cultures than are represented at the United Nations. Followers worship in the vernacular. Aborigines taking a communion bread of damper made in the red dust in Broome, Ethiopians chanting a wail in a corner of Africa that knew the Roman Empire, Guatemalans shaking incense over outdoor offerings and the English buying *The Tablet* after Sunday Mass in Westminster Cathedral are equal parts of the whole. In the small Carmelite community in Kew, Melbourne, which consists of around thirty women, eight different ethnic groups are represented, including Vietnamese, Italian and Tongan. Their daily rituals, beginning at 5.30 am and ending at 11.00 pm, are governed by a rule laid down in Spain and inspired by the solitary prayer of the Prophet Elijah. Their chants are full of the psalms of the Israelites and their 'Holy Father', who is Polish, lives in Rome. To Lilah, looking at Carmel, the community is held together by the stability of its ancient rule but it also reflects the national character.

My first interview was in 1969. I entered the next year. The only change that has occurred in Carmel since I entered is what is happening in Australian society and that which has been ordained by the Council of Vatican II. Australian society is fast becoming multicultural. Therefore any healthy religious community should also. Carmel reflects this. There are virtually eight different nationalities living under the same roof now.

And it is not all one way. In 1982 a small Carmelite community from Kew began a five year experimental occupation of an abandoned monastery 25 kilometres from Florence. The community had been invited by the Archbishop of Florence to revive the shrine, deserted since the upheavals of the Napoleonic Wars. The monastery, built in the fifteenth century, was uninhabitable, with primitive plumbing, no heating and a roof that leaked. The Carmelites are still there. Five Australian nuns have restored the derelict monastery, created a workable garden and are now very much part of the Tuscan landscape. Only one of the nuns sent from Kew had been outside Australia before they left. Now they get visits from prominent and ordinary Australians alike. Among the better known have been Sir Ninian and Lady Stephen and Sir James Gobbo of the Victorian Supreme Court. In 1988 they were visited by expatriate writer Desmond O'Grady who wrote a feature piece on the monastery for Fairfax's *Good Weekend*. But the nuns have also merged very successfully with the local culture and do not wish to be known simply as 'Australians in Tuscany' like some of their neighbours. They chant their daily office and masses in Italian and they have built a strong rapport as a service for the local Catholic community.

When Lilah left her house in Rathdowne Street, legally she still owned it. For a time her most valuable belongings were stored in the event of her leaving Carmel before taking final vows, others she left with friends on the understanding that they could keep them and there were some she simply gave away. Her 1888 edition of Cardinal Wiseman's lectures on 'the principal doctrines and practices of the Catholic Church' still occupies a small space on my library shelves. Her cat was adopted out, the VW Beetle, Lady Jane, became mine and Bertha, my old Prefect, went off to Judy and Joe to become the 'bionic Bertha' when parts from their even older Prefect were used as transplant material to prolong her life. Our friendship chain had developed very quickly into an occasional mutual help group. When Judy and Joe needed a temporary loan to bridge a gap in finance for a home, Lilah helped them out. Similarly there was an unspoken understanding that although Lilah had no family in Australia she could rely on friends if she ever changed her mind and 'came out'.

In 1982 Hyland productions for Network 10 Australia produced a documentary on the Carmelite community at Kew. It coincided with the fourth centenary of the death of St Teresa of Avila. The film charted one day's rhythms for the nuns, beginning before dawn as they left their rooms (bare except for table, chair, bed and crucifix on the wall) and moved along the corridors in silence to the chapel. As they assemble they walk in file chanting psalms in the plainsong of the medieval church. It was amusing to recall, as I watched the program, that at Rathdowne Street Lilah had often given hilarious renditions of the English traffic and road rules sung to the dips and rises of Gregorian chant. It had been the only way she had managed to learn them all for her driving test.

The *I Want To Be A Nun* documentary was screened on Australian television in prime viewing time over an hour and was intersected by advertisements in lurid colour offering all manner of tempting buys and tries. In ten minute segments of narrative, the everyday lives of the Carmelites were explored: praying, meditating in silence, singing in choir, undergoing a regular meeting in the Chapter Room for the 'accusation of faults', working in groups in the garden or in the laboratory making skin care products called 'Monastique' and 'Cardinal', playing tennis on rare feast day holidays in ankle length brown tunics, veils and plain white tennis shoes (no Reeboks) and taking vows of poverty, chastity and obedience. In between, Richard Gere carried off Debra Winger in a clip from *An Officer and A Gentleman*, an actress model baring everything from the shoulders up washed her hair to recommend the use of a new organic shampoo, steamy scenes from *Return To Eden* advertised a three part blockbuster coming soon and the robots of *Star Wars* flashed briefly across the screen. It was culture shock at every advertising break. Where, one might have asked, was 'one Australia'?

Even in an enclosed monastery the world cannot be completely shut out. Inside the Carmelite chapel the visitor comes face to face with an ornate temple of light centred on a marble canopy or dome above the altar, twelve steps up from the wooden and wicker chairs where the public can join with the community for mass. Level with the altar, a ceiling to floor door slides open to connect the community's interior chamber with the main altar. The visitor looks up and watches the nuns just visible at the massive opening. This is no everyday experience. Yet the Carmelite community is made up of women who spend hours every day praying for the needs of the world they have left.

Lilah has been part of Carmel for twenty-two years. As a national experience it is a rare one, even rarer than Lily's life among the small Chinese community of Cairns. I asked Lilah what she felt about being Australian after twenty-eight years, more than half her life.

Australia is the country I would give my first allegiance to, without any shadow of doubt. South Africa technically was my first nationality. And my Australian citizenship does not protect me against the laws of South Africa. But I refuse to be called a South African. I just feel a great pity for the country and I pray for it. Actually my spiritual roots are Australian. I worked out that they go back to the first hierarchy in Australia as my grandfather was baptised in Birmingham by Bishop Ullathorne, who as you know was the first Vicar General of Australia in 1832.

When I laughed at the coincidence of her discovery and joked that becoming Australian must have been preordained, fated by the hand of the Bishop, Lilah was not so easily amused. For a moment her English Catholicism flickered just a little as she replied, 'No. It was the will of God'.

Nhung and Phi

WHEN I went to pick up a briefcase at the ANZ Bank on Canberra's London Circuit it suddenly hit me that Nhung had a double life. And so did a lot of Australians. She was sitting at her computer terminal outside the manager's door next to a line of other desks and she didn't see me at first. In the bank's regulation uniform she looked just like all the other bank employees. But that was only one Nhung. The other one belonged inside a tale of hardship and horror experienced long before settling in suburban Florey.

Nhung came to Australia from Saigon in 1979. There are now thousands like her in offices and workplaces, in shops and schools. Nhung came with her slightly younger sister Phi who lives in Melbourne. Phi also works in a bank. Nhung is married and Phi will be married at Easter. They have two other sisters and a mother in Australia. All are naturalised

Australians. Nhung's husband Hai is one of a family of ten children most of whom now live outside Vietnam. Nhung and Phi have bought their own homes. They have been to university in Australia. They swim and ski during holidays and each owns spoilt pure-bred family dogs. Their mother spends a lot of her day talking to friends on the telephone. Except for their names they exemplify middle Australia.

Florey is one of the newer Canberra suburbs named after the man who invented penicillin. We took Belconnen Way and Coulter Drive and were soon there on Canberra's model freeways. If you are looking for an Australian ethnic ghetto you won't find it in Florey. It's as Australian as a modern version of Dame Edna's Moonee Ponds. Nhung and Hai have a piece of subdivided suburbia that slopes at the back, and there is a view of the lights and houses of nearby Page where we drove to eat at yet another Vietnamese restaurant doing a roaring trade mid-week in a local shopping centre. Our group of seven included Larissa, a German exchange student from Frankfurt, who discovered halfway through the meal that she lived in the same town as Hai's brother. The map of the Vietnamese exodus touches most corners of the globe.

Nhung and Phi joined the family just over a decade ago when they went to live with my mother not long after arriving in Australia. Their experience recalls Judy's story more than twenty years before. They were refugees from an international trouble spot and an Australian family took them in. They spoke hardly any English and they had only the bare necessities for belongings. You couldn't start with much less. After only one year they found a place of their own and shortly after that their next sister and cousins joined them. Before long their mother and the last sister came in a phenomenon of chain migration. Nhung's mother was so adept at organising her own family to leave Vietnam that by the time her turn came she knew the ropes so well she became her group's leader organising the whole getaway.

I spoke to Phi at a far corner table in the Kym-2, an up market Vietnamese restaurant in Victoria Street, Richmond, Melbourne's little Vietnam. My mother and Phi's fiancé, Hanh, ordered the meal at another table across the room. Phi spoke over the background noise into my portable tape recorder, her accented English reviewing escape, refugee camps and racial prejudice. Around us the waiters moved back and forth from the yuppy cosmopolitan bar in the centre of the room and customers drifted in to fill up the tables. It was hardly an ideal place for a recording but Phi had insisted on going to the restaurant because she thought her dogs would make too much noise at home. I looked Nhung up later and put the two stories together. They fitted like a matched pair.

The Vietnam War divided the world for a decade and was the single most polarising event of the second half of the twentieth century. When Nhung was ten years old in Saigon, Dr Jim Cairns led tens of thousands of demonstrators into the streets of Melbourne to bring city life to a halt in a sit down protest at 'US Imperialism' which they believed was destroying South Vietnam. In 1975 when the war ended, the North Vietnamese claimed victory in Soviet tanks which crunched through the streets of Saigon while in the United States Hollywood celebrities like Jane and Peter Fonda celebrated. The television world which had sent back graphic pictures of napalmed babies and last minute evacuations from South Vietnam had left a picture of horror in most living rooms. So I asked Nhung about her experiences of the war. Nhung was born in 1960. Her reply wasn't quite what I had expected.

When I grew up I didn't know much about what the outside looked like. All I knew was school, Mum waiting with dinner, there was always food and a nice warm house. I also liked the students in my school.

For Nhung and Phi and their family, life became harder after the war ended. This was not something that those in the West who had protested against the war readily understood. In their minds, come the peace all was supposed to be happiness in the Hanoi ruled republic. Gough Whitlam, when Opposition Leader, expressed his disappointment at any criticism of Vietnam over the plight of many fleeing the country as refugees. After a visit to Hanoi in November 1978, Mr Whitlam wrote in *The National Times* that he found Vietnam to be 'Spartan-disciplined, austere but strangely wholesome' and that in Hanoi 'The streets are lined with trees which meet overhead. There are pleasant lakes and gardens'.[1] A similar inability to understand why any Vietnamese might risk death to leave was evident in Labor figure Brian Burke's comments in Perth in July 1978 when he said, 'It is very strange that these so-called refugees are able, in some cases, to commandeer boats—at least in one case by force—and that they should all be leaving after the end of the Vietnam war. In my opinion any non-genuine refugee should be returned'.[2]

Nhung and Phi's father, a jeweller by trade, had been in the South Vietnamese Army, but he was not important enough to cause the family any special discrimination. Even so he was sent to a re-education camp. When the girls were still young he left them and their mother got a divorce. Under the Communist system Vietnam had become a police state. People lived in fear of offending the government. As in all Communist systems it wasn't long before you couldn't trust your neighbours some of whom had become the most effective State spies. There were curfews and limits on travel within Vietnam. No one could leave. And in the school holidays there were work camps that forced students into the fields to work. They rode their own bikes to get there. Phi remembers the camps vividly.

It was horrible working on the farms. You had to go for two weeks in the mud, whatever. We planted things and dug in the mud. We slept with the mud still on our feet. It was a couple of hours drive from Saigon and we had to bring our own food. They paid us nothing. We worked from early in the morning to late at night. There were no facilities.

It was their mother who pushed Nhung and Phi to escape. She was an avid anti-Communist and Nhung remembers her claiming to be able to point out 'Communists' in the streets. To Nhung's mother the Communist north represented a backward anti-life and she was determined her children would not have to be part of it. Her plan was to get the whole family out of Vietnam. It was a dangerous step and if they all went together and were caught the whole family would be trapped with no one on the outside to help them get free. If their mother stayed back she could buy their freedom on the black market if they were caught. She had learnt this from previous failures.

There were many attempts at escape before Nhung and

Phi made it. At first the mother arranged for just Nhung to go. This came to nothing after the plan was disbanded when it proved unsafe. The members of the group were left to find their own way home without being caught. Nhung can't remember how she got back. The second time Nhung did get caught but was eventually allowed to go home. Then the mother tried to arrange for the whole family to go with uncles, aunts and cousins in a group of fifteen. Again they failed. The agent took their money and left Vietnam without them. Nhung was sent out as a scout to ask why they had not been picked up. It was too late. The boat had left. Each time an attempt failed they lost the money that had been paid for the escape. 'It was heaps', says Nhung.

The desperate urge to escape was real enough. Many suffered direct persecution and labour camp torture. Others, like the Vietnamese Buddhists who had protested against the Thieu Government before the Communist takeover, now were denied their most important freedoms. One Buddhist, named Thien Quang, who had escaped Vietnam in 1979, told the *New York Times*, 'Under Thieu, we were only protesting against corruption. Now, under Communism we cannot exist at all'.[3]

During 1979 a row broke out between the two grand ladies of the Vietnam protest movement—Joan Baez and Jane Fonda. Joan Baez began the clash by going public on her change of mind over Vietnam. Under the auspices of Humanitas, her organisation formed to investigate human rights violations worldwide, she had discovered countless stories of repression in Vietnam. Her officer, Jeanetta Sagan, reported that all witnesses she had interviewed in France, whether refugees or journalists who had visited Vietnam or religious figures, told the same story. The stories formed a picture of 200 000 political prisoners being starved and tortured in camps. Jane Fonda angrily denied the reports and defended the Hanoi regime. A month later Jane herself had backed down and was condemning the Vietnamese Government for the plight of Chinese Vietnamese and she went on to say, 'I very much condemn the fact that there are violations of civil liberties'. There could be no doubt any longer.

Nhung's mother, however, had not lost her livelihood under the Communists. After her divorce she had kept her family by running what Phi describes as a milk bar, a corner shop above which the family lived. A second business in the rag trade helped add to the family income. When the Communists came to power Nhung and Phi's mother kept on quietly working at her non-political craft of sewing and built a steady business subcontracting other women to make school uniforms for the government. With something of an ironic twist it brought her the income that paid the successive boatmen who promised to take the family to freedom. Nhung's mother had an urge to leave that came from her fear of what the future under Communism meant for her children. She heard about what had happened to others and resolved that it would not happen to her family. Nhung: *I was at high school. Mum reckoned that Communism was not a very good future. She believed that kids who grew up as Communists were damaged. It didn't matter how hard you tried you would get nowhere even after education. She believed that her money for the escape was for our future.*

The pitiful scenes of Vietnamese boat people in the 1970s and 1980s began soon after the Communist takeover. In Australia Gough Whitlam, who was Prime Minister when Saigon fell, argued in Cabinet against taking any 'Vietnamese Balts' fleeing from an occupying Communist army. A year after the fall of Saigon, with Malcolm Fraser's Coalition Government newly installed, the first Vietnamese boat people began to arrive on the northern coast of Australia. By 1979 the number of refugees in south-east Asian camps was 200 000. Many were ethnic Chinese whom the Vietnamese Government had forced out. Between 1975 and 1985, 79 000 Vietnamese came to Australia. About half were ethnic Vietnamese like Nhung and Phi and the rest were Chinese Vietnamese. Their stories have a familiar, at times grisly, flavour. For every two Vietnamese refugees who survived one did not. Bruce Grant points out in *The Boat People: An Age Investigation* that there is strong evidence to suggest that in 1978 and 1979 the Hanoi Government was encouraging the flight of boat people and operating much of the trafficking itself through clandestine government agents. Passages for adults averaged between $2400 and $3000 Australian (in gold) and half that for a child. At the time an Australian family car cost about $9000.

Nhung is uncertain how much money her mother had to pay. She remembers it varied according to how much the trafficker thought you could afford. Some escapees were lucky to get away by paying very little. Her mother was told a trip could be organised for Nhung and Phi. They would be looked after. She paid the money. Then they waited for the pick-up. Nhung describes what happened.

We were picked up by a small motor bike. The driver took us to a river which was a sort of port. We had to wear simple clothes so we wouldn't be recognised. We had to look poor and ragged. The man told my mum that we would get a little boat and it would take us out to the ocean and swap us onto a big boat. But instead they picked us up and dropped us on land near a forest and left us for three nights. There was nothing. Not a hut. We had to hide from some logging men. I cried. Phi cried too. It was about two hours from Saigon and not far from the sea. What they were doing was rounding up some other people and it was not safe to bring us all at once.

They eventually had some company as more people were dropped off. One was an older man who had been released from a re-education camp. They each slept for an hour at a time while someone kept watch. Nhung remembers the mosquitos which were so bad she had to fan them away from Phi so she could sleep. There was some water to drink and some food at lunch time. Eventually there were enough passengers to satisfy the trafficker and the boat left, not a big one as promised but a small one, with 27 people aboard.

That little boat was eleven metres long and about two and a half metres wide. We got on and tried to pretend it was a fishing boat. Nhung and I had one friend on board and we knew his cousin who was organising the trip. Mostly they were young people and young men who did not want to do duty work such as going in the army. It was the last resort to go in the army. We went to Malaysia.

When you ask someone to recount such a traumatic and uncertain experience there are a lot of gaps. Phi was very sick and vomited for three days. They were at sea for seven days. Nhung managed to find Phi a spot below deck where she could lie down. Nhung recollects that at times Phi became unconscious. When I talked to Phi she remembered little except that the water they were offered was bad. With dictatorial control the leader of the group insisted that all on board must not move from the spaces allotted to them. An American ship stopped to offer assistance and gave them food, water, petrol and a compass. A doctor came on board ('he was so fat', says Nhung) and squeezed into the engine room to help with Phi. Her hand was also bleeding from being caught by the machinery. Nhung can recall only these few details. She has no idea of how they kept clean, urinated or managed with the others in such a cramped space. She remembers some arguments and fist fights but her mind has blocked a lot out. She just says it was awful. The voyage could have been much worse. They were travelling in May and were lucky. In the following month of June thousands died in the monsoonal weather. For a time their mother thought they were dead when she didn't hear from them.

In 1978 and 1979 Vietnamese boat people became a blot on the South China Sea. They were without any international status and if picked up by a passing ship immediately became the responsibility of the country to which the ship belonged. Many vessels witnessing the plight of these unfortunate people crowded into smelly leaky boats—families with small children, pregnant women, starved and sick flotsam on the ocean—could not just sail on although others did. Captain Healey Martin from Northern Ireland was one who could not sail by. He picked up a group of some 600 Vietnamese on his way to Hong Kong from Bangkok. The refugees were nearly out of water, fuel and food. They had just buried five babies at sea. The boat was close to sinking. Captain Martin, assisted by his wife and a crew of Indians, Britons and two Australians, set about helping the sad ragged group on board. Shortly after they picked up another 300 people, mostly women and children, from a second boat.

The rescue created a storm in the British House of Commons when Margaret Thatcher's Conservatives refused to honour the undertaking of the previous Labour Government that refugees picked up at sea would be given asylum in Britain. The case, which also widened when another British ship picked up a group of refugees, was finally resolved by a Conservative backdown. However, the trouble the dispute caused for the shipping company and the unfortunate captains was a warning to future seamen not to get involved with boat people.

Many, like the American ship that passed Nhung and Phi, helped by giving supplies of food and fuel and even medicine. But that was about it. By the late 1980s journalists were reporting compassion burnout. William Shawcross writing in *The Spectator* in June 1989 focused on the lack of concern saying, 'Thousands upon thousands of boat people are still pouring out of Vietnam and across the South China Sea. They are being murdered, raped, pillaged, locked in camps and cages. And almost nothing is being said'.[4] In the Gulf of Thailand pirates plied their foul trade, robbing and raping the Vietnamese, unstopped for a decade. By the late 1980s there were reports that Thai fishermen no longer fished in the Gulf because their nets were so often ruined by the wrecks in the waters and they pulled up bodies with the fish. In 1989 the Hong Kong Government sent back its first plane load of Vietnamese refugees from one of its many refugee camps. The argument given new favour was that these refugees were only 'economic' refugees. Meanwhile in the United States it was reported that 'Hanoi Jane' (the name given to Jane Fonda after she visited North Vietnam during the war) was announcing her separation from husband Tom Hayden, her partner in radical politics since the 1960s. The separation was described as a political as well as a marriage break-up and possibly the nail in the coffin of 'sixties politics.

The most successful passage to freedom for the boat people was the route down the southern tip of Vietnam and out across the South China Sea to the eastern coast of Malaysia. As a result the coastal towns on the Malay peninsula quickly saw an invasion of small boats filled with wretched people. By 1979 the coast guard and the villagers of Malaysia were gaining an unpleasant reputation for their tactics designed to deter refugee boat people from landing. The racial and diplomatic upheaval the Vietnamese boat people caused for Malaysia is highlighted in Blanche d'Alpuget's novel *Turtle Beach*. Once the refugees were ashore the host country was supposed to accept responsibility for them so the practice soon grew of towing refugee boats out to sea to prevent them from landing. The boat that Nhung and her sister were on was towed away at first.

*So many Vietnamese had come out that the Malaysian
people were just fed up with us. What they did was push
people out to sea or put them in another boat that would
not sink. Our boat was broken in the middle and we
were lucky because the Malaysians transferred us to
another boat. The next time the sea police tried to send
us away, to pull us out; but we said we cannot go any
more and we just stopped. The leader took our side and
we got ashore. It was a little town and we stayed there
for about two months. I didn't mind it there. Then they
said we had to move to a proper place where there was
information about refugees. They moved us to a big sports
oval where there were thousands of refugees. We were the
last to arrive there.*

Refugee camps are smelly undignified places where
people idle away their time living in makeshift squats while
they are 'processed'. Nhung and Phi were at first forced to
share space at the sports oval with one other group. The
group managed in a single tent next to the toilets. The stench
was sickening. It poured with rain and the tent leaked. When
Nhung and Phi were noticed by a Chinese Vietnamese lady
she took pity on them and gave them shelter with her large
family at the other end of the oval. Today she keeps in touch
with Nhung and Phi from her home in Switzerland. When
the camp was disbanded just two weeks later, the inmates
were moved to Malaysia's international refugee camp on
Pulau Tengah, near Mersing, Johor. Nhung and Phi spent
eight months there.

During Melbourne summers a few years after Nhung and
Phi arrived in Australia they sometimes came over to swim
while we cooked a barbecue or spread out food in the shade
under an enormous cypress tree. Most of the visitors would
desert the salty chlorine after the customary cool down and
spend time poolside chatting, drinking or sunbaking. But
Nhung would stay in the water, a sleek black blob
breaststroking the ten metres up and the ten metres down
for half an hour at a time. Her action was so leisurely and
precise she hardly made a ripple on the surface and eventually we would forget what she was doing. She told me it was
something she had become addicted to on the island in

Malaysia where she swam for hours in the sea to keep occupied and relax from her worries.

The world is now dotted with refugee camps. Dignitaries visit them, guerillas shell them, in Hong Kong they are forcibly emptied. They are no-man's lands of hope. Australian refugee camps house Chinese and Cambodian boat people who are photographed by occasional press teams as governments, bureaucrats and lawyers discuss their cases. In Thailand the refugee camps of Cambodians became so entwined with the local scenery, with their thatched huts, dusty streets and population of over 200 000 people, that they won the euphemistic title of border camps. Refugee camps quickly become official settlements invaded by Red Cross workers. They are rough shanty communities full of lost people. In wealthy Hong Kong or Australia they take on the appearance of internment camps surrounded by cyclone fences trimmed with escape-proof barbed wire at the top. All camps contain good and bad as in any settlement. And the occupants are all desperate to get away but rarely to go back home.

Nhung and Phi have mostly positive recollections of their time on the refugee island. Memory has softened with their successful resettlement in Australia. And these days eight months probably does not seem very long. Their experiences were those of anxiety and deprivation but they were never assaulted or abused like many. Nhung looks back on the period.

I think I enjoyed it there. It was a sort of a holiday and I was always swimming. I learnt some English, I was a Girl Guide leader looking after the cubs and I helped in the library. I had a routine and kept busy. I also helped with work for the international office there. Phi worked at the office in the library. One of the nuns who came to the island brought books in English and Phi was responsible for selling them to the whole island. She gave Phi a commission. She brought about 200 books a month. It wasn't many. There were 12 000 people there. Some would ask Phi to hold books for them. I also did the mail. Mail came from everywhere to that camp. Everybody wanted their mail—parents, sisters, brothers.

But Phi can remember other scenes too, the brutality dished out to others.

The Malaysian soldiers, they were really mean. I'd seen things. They were supposed to look after us. I don't know about rape. It's possible the girls never raised a strong voice. I don't know. But they hit the men. If they didn't like someone's work they would call him up to the office and beat him up. I worked for them alright. At our first camp there was no fence and we didn't have enough food. People who had some money went out to buy food from the town. When they got back they were beaten. When we left to go to Pulau Tengah the Malaysians wouldn't let those people go.

Back home in Vietnam Nhung and Phi's mother was having a hard time. While they were left to wait, abandoned in the forest, she thought they were safely away on a ship. A day after they went, she was taken to the police station and questioned. Her neighbours had reported her. I asked Nhung why the neighbours would do that, and if they were bribed. She said it was just a case of jealousy like dobbing in a person for cheating on social welfare payments in Australia. Nhung's mother told the police that the girls were visiting relatives in the country. It seemed to pass for the truth. But the family got a red mark stamped on their papers all the same. The red mark meant that members of the family were treated as second class citizens at the government shops, and certain foodstuffs or goods were not available to them. Families whose children had escaped were happy to suffer the red mark if their children were safely out of Vietnam.

When word from Nhung and Phi did not come weeks after they had left, the mother feared the worst. She heard rumours that they had not got away safely and were in fact in a prison camp in the countryside away from Saigon. The organiser of the boat which took Nhung and Phi had promised their mother that he would stay with them on the voyage but he turned up in Saigon after three days. She was shocked to see him. He assured her all was fine but she still wasn't convinced. She couldn't sleep for worry. At last, word came from America that her daughters were alive and safe. In the camp in Malaysia Nhung had sent a message out with someone who was leaving.

She found out we were alive months after we left Vietnam. We sent our message with someone who was going to America and they sent a telex to our mum. In the camp people who were leaving could not take all the letters that had to be sent, there were so many. So people gave addresses to the ones that were leaving and they would pass a message on to the relatives in Vietnam. When my sister Xuan came out she was able to telex my mum after a week, from Singapore. But we had no facility.

Both Nhung and Phi believe that they came to Australia partly because they were single women. Word about at the time in the selection queues was that the Australian authorities had found they needed to balance the intake of single Vietnamese men with some women. Around 57 per cent of the intake at that time were single men. Nhung and her sister really wanted to go to the United States.

I was in the camp and I had no idea which country I was going to live in. When we left Mum said, 'It is no matter where you are as long as you get out of the country. Go to any country that accepts you. You will get a good education and have a good future. I am happy'. Everybody wanted to go to America. I don't know why. Even me and Phi. We just followed the others. In the camp we talked to people and they said it was getting harder to go to America. You had to have relatives there or your father had to be involved in the war before 1975. We tried applying but we were told we were too young and did not have our parents. Then others told us that Australia was the best place to settle for good. It was a quiet country, an island. We didn't even know how to find it on a map. So we chose Australia. But we arrived just after the Australian immigration people had been to our island. We had to wait six months till they came back again. Then they called us for an interview and I went. I learned some English every day so that I could talk a little at the interview. Some of my friends in the office where we worked helped us to practise the sort of

*things that we would be asked. That gave us an idea
what to talk about.*

The day Nhung and Phi arrived in Australia, 30 April 1980,
was the fifth anniversary of the fall of Saigon. They knew a
little English but had only the clothes they wore. The rings
their mother had given them when they left home had long
since been stolen. Phi recalls the fate of the rings.

*We owned nothing except the clothes we had been given
by the Red Cross and at the refugee centres. Mum gave
us some rings to sell when we left so we might have some
money, but the owner of the boat took them before we got
on board. He spoke to all of us and said anything we
had he wanted. He took the rings. What the others did I
don't know. He was greedy. Just making money out of
refugees.*

Nhung and Phi were an exotic but waif-like deposit when
they found themselves gathered up by an Australian family
not long after their arrival at the Nunawading hostel. Gwen,
their foster mother, had brought up seven children of her
own. Most had left home so there was room for a couple
more. She heard about Nhung and Phi from the St Vincent
de Paul Society, an auxiliary arm of Catholic charitable work.
One by one the family members came by to meet Nhung and
Phi and in time they filled their spaces in the family photo
albums.

Before long Nhung and Phi were contacted by their sister
Xuan and some cousins, the first of their family needing a
sponsor to migrate to Australia. We began arranging to make
room for them at my home. Then Nhung and Phi found work.
With the offer of an old house and a reduced rent they soon
became eligible to sponsor the cousins themselves. The St
Vincent de Paul Society helped again, furnishing the house.
And Gwen was never far away, helping out as needed.

When I first knew Nhung and Phi we couldn't say much
to one another. They seemed small and frail and vulnerable.
Their hurdles seemed immense. But their assimilation had
been made easier by the 1978 Galbally Report on migrant
programs and services. The recommendations of the report
were adopted by the Fraser Government in the same year.
Non-English-speaking immigrants like Nhung and Phi had the

support of government-sponsored community language programs and a broadened commitment to special assistance in
learning to speak English. There were commitments to equal
opportunity in the work place and in education. The first
step, Phi says, was to learn English.

*The most difficult thing was to learn English, I suppose,
to understand people and to know what to do. We went
to classes for six months in Box Hill. One does classes not
courses in English there. Then I went straight on to do
the Accounting Certificate at the Box Hill Tech. I did that
for a year and then I got a job as a bank clerk. After my
Accounting Certificate I enrolled part time immediately
for my Computer Science degree. It took six years.*

There are many myths about non-English-speaking
immigrants and Vietnamese refugees in particular. Most
Vietnamese refugees do not, as believed, arrive with lots of
gold. Most arrive like Nhung and Phi did, with nothing.
Cabramatta in western Sydney and the Housing Commission
flats in Melbourne's inner suburb Richmond, where many
Vietnamese can be found, are not evidence of millionaire
settlements but racy, vibrant market places.

When Phi found a job after a year in Australia she disputed
the other general belief that non-English-speaking immigrants
are always a drain on Australian taxpayers. And so did Nhung
who also found a job in a bank with only nine units of her
Accounting course finished. Perhaps they are an example of
the type of employee described by the English-born assistant
manager of Sydney's Haymarket branch of the Commonwealth Bank. In 1987 he told the *Sydney Morning Herald*
that, while Asian employees were treated like anyone else,
their 'actual standard and attitudes to their work is absolutely
tremendous' and that from the group perspective 'their per-
formance is higher than non-Asians. Their attitude to their
job, and their commitment, is absolutely tremendous'.[5] Nhung
talks about getting her bank job.

*My English improved a lot in 1981. It wasn't very
excellent but I could be understood. I read the newspaper
and saw an ad for a job in banking. I applied. They
asked me, 'What do you know about banking?'. I told
them I had nearly finished my Accounting course. They*

*said, 'Well, how about an interview?'. And then I went
for an interview. The man was Irish. I still can remember
him. He interviewed me and said, 'Why do you want to
work in a bank? You have got no experience'. I said that
I could do any job in the bank. He said, 'What makes
you go to work? Why don't you study at Tech? You need
to finish the course and you have done very well'. My
references from my Accounting teacher said I had picked
it up very quickly. I told him that I had no parents in
Australia and I wanted to earn a living. I needed a job
first. I said that if he employed me I would work part
time and continue my education. He liked me and gave
me the job in two days. It was at the ANZ Bank in
Camberwell. Phi got her job two weeks before me in the
ANZ in Collins Place.*

This was a remarkable achievement for both girls. In
personality they are very different. Nhung is the practical one
and vivaciously outgoing. Phi is quieter but has an inner
determination and will. As Rita understood, the problem of
language depends greatly on the fearlessness of the user.
Stumble, fall and get back up again is the successful migrant's
pattern. Nhung explains how she and Phi were helped.

*When I stayed with Gwen I was lucky because I learnt
English very quickly. A lot of people who came out at the
same time as me didn't get a job that quick. They still
had to learn English and were struggling with Uni. Now
Phi and I talk about how quick Gwen sounded when she
first talked to us. We couldn't understand her she talked
so fast. She would say, 'Listen girls, listen to me'. She was
very patient and she explained it to us. She put the TV
on in the morning and would say, 'That program is for
kids but you can listen'. She was a teacher and we
learnt. When I see her now she doesn't talk fast at all.*

Mixing daily with an Australian family did make a difference. Cam Nguyen, writing in *Without Prejudice* in 1990,
explained why Vietnamese have a particular difficulty in
learning English:

Vietnamese is a tonal language with numerous words of
Chinese origin. Just as it takes a native English speaker much

longer (more than twice as long according to the US State Department) to acquire a good working knowledge of Chinese or Vietnamese than say, Dutch or German, so it takes Vietnamese much longer to learn English than speakers of an Indo–European language.[6]

Looked at from the other way round, however, Nhung and Phi along with thousands of first and second generation Australians, like Rita and her children, are revolutionising Australian society. Language maintenance among Vietnamese, Italian, Greek and Chinese Australians is very high. There are now 60 000 speakers of Vietnamese and 170 000 with a Chinese language and culture who are long term Australians. Hundreds of thousands of others have backgrounds and languages from the Middle East and Europe. Australia, for so long insulated from foreign languages by distance and official policy, now is a multilingual society.

Judy found it was hard work learning English but her finished product is very much that of the polished vowels she yearned for. Nhung and Phi have mastered English very well but they still have strong accents that will probably never change.

As a group among newly arrived immigrants the Vietnamese have not been as successful as Nhung and Phi in finding work. Overall they have experienced higher than average rates of unemployment. Their difficulties have been exacerbated by the failure of Australian professional groups to recognise foreign qualifications, a problem for many European migrants too. And there were other problems such as union resentment coming from suspicion about the sudden influx of Vietnamese who were being forced into unskilled factory work at a time when such jobs were becoming scarce. Michael Quinlan and Constance Lever-Tracy point out in *Australia and Immigration—able to grow?* that Vietnamese immigrants were also under suspicion from unionists through the assumption that they had 'right wing' political leanings, as well as through their portrayal in the media as being 'preferred by employers because of their aggressive job seeking and diligence as workers'.[7]

In Tim Winton's *Scission*, a collection of short stories about Australia, one story titled 'The Oppressed' is an impressionistic piece about two Australians who have befriended a Vietnamese migrant. It depicts seemingly unbridgeable gaps of experience between the friends even though the bonds are strong. Told from the perspective of the Vietnamese refugee, Quoi, the story is intersected with flashes of thought that move between confusion and nightmares he cannot share with his Australian friends. Quoi forms a view of them that they are '. . .concerned about politics, but only of a sort', and think 'in fiery, innocent terms—in principles'. For him politics is 'how much food and who will die . . . without time to wield these principles, only a numbness'.[8]

Among refugee immigrants, in particular those from Indo-China but by no means exclusively, there are great extremes in the torment that they bring with them. Many have known brutal internment, some torture; others have no idea where family and loved ones are or if they are still alive, many have suffered agonising and perilous voyages. The remarkable thing is that so many have been successful settlers, urged on by the hard-edged realities perhaps. Those who cannot cope find their way to centres like STARTTS (Service for the Treatment and Rehabilitation of Torture and Trauma Survivors) which operates from Fairfield, a suburb in Sydney. Many of the counsellors are people who have recovered from torments themselves and they say that one of the biggest problems is isolation and a fear of the intimidating newness of a foreign country. Nhung and Phi have always appeared unscarred by their escape and refugee experience, but as their English improved they began to reveal some of the uglier moments for them and others. Talking about their experiences helped.

Nhung is proud of the fact that she and Phi have both carried the flag for the Vietnamese contingent in the Anzac Day march in Melbourne. Phi in 1982, Nhung in 1983. Five hundred and four Australians were killed in the Vietnam war. But the survivors became casualties too. The widow of the first combat soldier to die in Vietnam spoke much later of how she soon learned not to tell people where he died, and made up stories that he had been killed in a road accident. It was not until 1987 that the Vietnam veterans, thanks mainly to the single-minded efforts of one veteran, got a welcome

home march in the streets of Sydney. After that the healing
process was under way.

On Saturday 3 October 1992, in Canberra, the Vietnam
Memorial commemorating the fallen in Vietnam was unveiled
and dedicated. Thousands filled the broad tracts of Anzac
Parade that runs between Parkes Way and the Canberra War
Memorial. In the seated audience were representatives of the
Vietnamese community in Australia, two wearing the yellow
robes of Buddhist monks. Those who gazed across the lake
at the distinctive outline of the old Parliament House were
reminded of the scenes of old scores. At the podium dignitaries spoke of honour, pride and burden. Prime Minister Paul
Keating, stopping just short of apology, lauded those killed
in the defence of 'freedom in Vietnam' and acknowledged
that they had now joined the exalted ranks of all who had
served in other wars for Australia. The Opposition leader,
John Hewson, echoed his sentiments. General Sir Thomas
Daly spoke passionately of the service that had been given
and of the veterans' return home to 'controversy, apathy and
sometimes worse'. A forest of newly planted trees moved
quietly in a light breeze near the Shrine of three truncated
white-grey slabs like giant tablets, half open, half closed,
around a wall-sized photo of a chopper rescuing Australian
soldiers in the field.

On the day the Memorial was dedicated a march past
rounded off the ceremony. It was a sentimental and proud
moment for those participating. The march went well over
time as battalion after battalion went by. It finished with a
mass contingent of Vietnamese ex-servicemen carrying the
Australian flag, who passed to a rousing welcome, closely
followed by the symbol of American presence everywhere in
the form of a long file of bikie servicemen on Harley David-
sons. To all present it marked the end of a long war.

Nhung and Phi are not particularly political. But they
belong to a group of migrants who are assumed to be
political because of their rejection of the Communist system,
by their having voted against it with their feet. As with all
other immigrant communities the Vietnamese have politically
active groups who send out newsletters and disseminate
political literature. It is unsurprisingly anti-Communist but not
clandestine. Like other migrants most Vietnamese are con-

cerned above all else for their families' well-being and about making a success of their new life.

An invitation to join a Vietnamese National Day in 1990 was a reminder of how diminished are the old issues even in the Vietnamese community. National Day celebrations attract large crowds and take place in suburban locations like the Civic Centre at Sydney's Bankstown. When we arrived the entrance lobby sported a table of Vietnamese literature but the real interest was in the singing and small opera items on stage, as well as the statements of support from senior Australians.

The specially invited guests included the local member, the ALP's John Newman, and Senator Peter Baume representing the Federal Liberal Opposition. As the concert progressed, lengthily outlined in both Vietnamese and English on the program, dances and songs in Vietnamese pieced together traditional stories. Then civic figures spoke of the warm relationship between the Vietnamese community and their adopted country. There was light relief when the microphone hiccupped and briefly played throbbing music from the Saturday night disco next door while one speaker was commending the way the Vietnamese had contributed to the Australian lifestyle. It was clear they had not quite mastered the Bankstown Civic Centre's electronics.

When they began their lives in Australia living with Australians Nhung and Phi had a head start. Some Vietnamese are gradually now recognising that they need to mix more with Australian friends. Interviewed for *Good Weekend* in 1989, Brisbane restaurant owner Nguyen Cang admitted that his family had begun to move out of their tight Vietnamese circle in order to become better adapted to their new society. Nhung and Phi had to move in reverse. They visited friends each week at the Nunawading hostel to keep in touch.

Gwen would drop Phi and me off there to say hello to all the people we knew. Some of the Vietnamese girls cooked at the hostel and we came for dinner. Later we met people at weddings. Everyone was at the wedding. That is the place to show off your dress, where single boys can meet the single girls. Just like a community but they invite everybody. Even if they only met you in a shop for

five minutes you got an invitation to the wedding the
next week. I met Hai at a wedding. I was the bridesmaid.

   Rita's daughter Anna believes that all children of immigrant parents reject their cultural origins for a time when
growing up. In her view it comes from trying to assimilate
and to become like everyone else. Then later the immigrant
background becomes a valuable enrichment. Nhung and Phi,
who came to Australia without parents, did not appear to go
through a stage of rejecting their Vietnamese culture. But
Nhung did admit to having a separate life with 'Australian'
friends. The photo of a skiing party among her collection
confirms this. In Canberra Nhung and Hai have mostly non-
Vietnamese friends. Phi also stresses that she is most
cosmopolitan.

To be honest I have more Australian friends than
Vietnamese friends. Once you go to work full time and
study part time you never have much time for your
friends except for workmates. I have made a lot of friends
through my work and my Vietnamese friends are mainly
people I met when I came to Australia or when we went
to school back then. And I had an Australian boyfriend
for seven years.

   The Vietnamese boat people were the first group of Asians
to benefit from the formal ending of the White Australia
Policy in 1973. Much of the policy had been repealed when
Harold Holt was Prime Minister but the final dismantling
came in the time of Gough Whitlam. However, immigration
from Asia was not encouraged by the Whitlam Government;
while it proclaimed an end to White Australia in theory, there
was little manifestation of an open door to Asian immigrants.
With the Fraser Government there was a recognition that
Australia must acknowledge a responsibility for the Indo-Chinese boat people if only because of Australia's part in the
Vietnam war.

   This was not a popular policy and the Australian community had mixed feelings about the intake of Vietnamese. A
poll reported in *The Age* in June 1979 showed only 23 per
cent in favour of continuing to accept Indo-Chinese refugees.
Bob Hawke, who as Prime Minister stood firm against racism
of any kind, was another who was not then ready for refugees

from Vietnam. In the 1977 Federal election campaign he tried as ACTU President to make an election issue out of media reports of the imminent arrival of a boatload of Vietnamese in Darwin. In his view refugees who 'simply landed on [our] doorstep' could not be accepted. During some heated debates in 1984 the Deputy Leader of the Liberal–National Coalition, John Howard, was able to use Bob Hawke's comments on the Vietnamese to good effect in Parliament. A few years later John Howard had changed tack and was making his own inflammatory statements about Asian immigration. Listening between the lines of John Howard's on-the-run remarks it seemed that it was Australia's large number of Vietnamese citizens who were bearing the brunt of the attack. Many like Phi felt the sting of racial prejudice for the first time since coming to Australia.

The first time I experienced racism was when John Howard was making some comments. I went to the city one day and this old man was holding a big board in front of me that said 'No Asians'. He did that to any Asians walking past at lunch time in the city. I had never struck that before. And my younger sister, Loan, had a similar experience. She went with one of her friends to the canteen in the city for lunch and this rude old man, who would have been in the Army because he wore all these medals, looked at Loan and said, 'You come from Vietnam? People over there eat dirt don't they?'.

Much of the argument over multiculturalism has centred on a view that 'separate' development is rampant in Australia and the community is dividing into ethnic ghettos. Ask those who argue this to name the ghettos and they usually have difficulty. But when areas of heavy Vietnamese settlement are singled out it is hard to justify the label of ghetto. Where is the poverty in these brash mercantile suburbs? They have become tourist attractions. Cabramatta in Sydney, often called Vietnamatta, is now a meeting spot for a hundred and one nationalities where the influx of new immigrants has transformed a drab outer suburb into a valuable business district. At weekends it can take fifteen minutes to get into the multistorey car park. And in Melbourne's Richmond a similar transformation has occurred. Its shopping district stretching along Victoria Street, only a few minutes from the central Melbourne business district, is mostly occupied by Vietnamese shops. Yet the area is only 15 per cent Vietnamese. It is multicultural like Cabramatta. Richmond's Mayor, Sang Nguyen, was one of a handful of selected Australians to go to Canberra in February 1992 to join in a lunch with the Queen.

Most Vietnamese do not live in the clusters of Cabramatta and Richmond. But they shop and eat there as the Chinese, like Lily and many other Asians, shop and eat in Chinatown. Gradually many non-Asian Australians are joining them. In Melbourne Phi shops in Victoria Street because it is cheap and she eats there a lot. The entrepreneurs among Australia's Asian immigrants have developed extensive food chains. As we ate our Vietnamese meal in Canberra's Page, Nhung's husband Hai told Larissa that his brother in Frankfurt has to eat potatoes because there is such a poor range of Vietnamese food in the shops there. In Australia, he maintains, the range of Vietnamese foodstuffs is equal to the best ever available in Vietnam.

In arguing against the government's immigration policy in 1987 Professor Geoffrey Blainey criticised the policy of selecting migrants from 'cultures which, in many ways, are considerably different from our own'. He was unspecific but the government's choice of Vietnamese was written everywhere between the lines. It is hard to agree with Professor Blainey when talking to Nhung or Phi or any of their family or friends. Like Hungarian Judy, Nhung and Phi grew up with no particular religion. Like Judy they have both become Catholics, as Nhung explains.

To be honest, when we grew up I didn't follow any religion at all. I wasn't Buddhist or Catholic at that time. My parents were nothing either. My mum's sister married a Catholic and she followed the Catholics. So my family was a bit Catholic. Then when I went to high school all my friends were Catholic and I remember my girl friend when I was about ten, she kept talking to me about God. She said, 'Nhung you pray and Maria will do this or this and so on'. So I went to church, not often but always at Christmas. On the refugee island half the island was Catholic. So all my new friends were Catholic again. I

*joined the Catholic choir. I could have become a Catholic
on the island if I wished but one of my friends said that
I should wait till I could do it nicely.*

Nhung and Phi were both baptised in Australia. On the
boat Phi remembers they prayed to 'Maria' and their prayers
were answered. It wasn't hard to believe in God after that.
But a little while ago Nhung had an exchange with her parish
priest whom she suspected of being Vietnamese.

*I think there is a Vietnamese priest at my parish in Page.
I went to confession maybe once or twice a year. Now we
sit face to face and I got a shock because I had never
done it before in my life. And he looked at me and said,
'How are you, girl?' And I said, 'Good, father.' He was
Asian but I didn't know if he was Vietnamese or not.
Then he asked me, 'Where do you come from, by the
way?' And I said, 'Vietnam, father.' And he said, 'Ah,
you're a Vietnamese girl.' I said, 'Yes, father.' And he
said, 'Oh, you got an Australian husband?' 'No father.'
'Who is your husband?' 'Vietnamese husband, father.'
And he said, 'Ah.' I didn't know how he judged me. I
didn't know him did I? He said, 'How long have you
lived in this area for?' I said, 'Five years, father.' 'You go
to this church?' 'Yes, father.' And I said to him, 'How
long have you been in this parish, father?' 'Three months.'
And then I said, 'Oh that is why when I last went to
Mass I didn't see you father.' I went home and said to
Hai, 'There is a Vietnamese father at the church. I am
not going to go there any longer'.*

In 1991 Nhung and Hai went back to Vietnam for a week.
They wanted to go for a longer holiday to Europe and had
saved hard. But Hai's father died just weeks before he was
due to come to Australia. He was going to be the last member
of the family to leave and his family were looking forward
to having him with them. So Hai was given the task of going
home to Ho Chi Minh City as a mark of respect for the family.
Nhung's feelings at losing her European holiday were very
mixed but afterwards she was pleased she had visited
'Saigon'. She found things different from when she had left,
not yet very prosperous but a city freed of a lot of its fears
and openly talking again. She saw her father as well.

Some among the older Vietnamese community can feel lonely in Australia and not very comfortable. Phi has noticed that Vietnamese Australians who sponsor older relatives for six month visits often find that the relatives are not comfortable in Australia and do not want to apply for permanent residence. For most people things are better now in Vietnam and the relatives can come for holidays and go back to a lifestyle they feel part of. In Australia they miss familiar things. In Vietnam they can lead a more active life. Phi's mother has some friends who came for a visit and took someone back with them. Sometimes Phi's mother, who is still very wary of the Communists, says she would like to go back to Vietnam to live when they are all married. Phi thinks her mother is joking and thinks she would miss her grandchildren. But Phi's mother is experiencing a familiar homesickness that afflicts all immigrants caught between two homes.

Nhung and Phi have been Australian citizens since 1982. They became citizens as soon as they were able to. All the family did the same. Nhung says they could hardly wait to 'get the certificate'. Both are qualified in Computer Science and Nhung is planning a future full of happy dreams.

Next year I am going to do Commerce at the ANU.
Although I am not sure because I am planning to have a
baby—so that is my dream. When I am sitting here in
ten years time I will be a lawyer or a good accountant. I
probably won't be at the bank anymore. It will be eleven
years in September since I started working in the bank.
And I want to earn heaps of money.

Phi also plans a broader career and is thinking of a small city take-away restaurant. As a force in Australian professional life they and their extended family are intimidating. In Hai's family all ten children have gone to university turning out engineers, computer scientists, one working in commerce and one on the way through dentistry at Sydney University. Phi's sister Xuan, another computer scientist, has married a young Vietnamese doctor who has two brothers in medicine (one a specialist) and another brother an engineer. Her other sister Loan is studying computer engineering. Hanh, Phi's fiancé, is a computer scientist who works in stockbroking.

All have been educated in Australia. By not recognising the professional qualifications of numerous Vietnamese, Australia has lost many of the best qualified refugees to the United States, Canada and France.

In 1980, at the refugee camp in Malaysia, Nhung and Phi each received a 'Letter of Appreciation' for their work with the United Nations High Commissioner for Refugees. In the letters, signed by Mr Joseph Paul for the UNHCR and the Chairman of the Administrative Committee of the Pulau Tengah Refugee Camp, Nhung and Phi from Boat No. SOS 27 were declared to have 'voluntarily contributed his/her time and effort for the development and welfare of this community'. It wasn't an elaborate reference but it was official.

As Nhung finished her interview, with the lights of Page a kilometre away in the background, she became reflective. It had been a long night. 'It's funny, looking into the past, Anne', she said. 'We were lucky. My family was lucky.'

Epilogue

Popular history in Australia shuns the rosy picture. The term 'lucky country' is an ironic one in the minds of the intellectual. Song writers, poets, historians and commentators draw an image of a man's own country. Maleness and masculinity saturate the icons. Women seem to have had only bit parts on the national stage and mateship is an all-male term.

Yet in 1992 when bureaucrats in the Reserve Bank of Australia decided to remove the portrait of Mrs Caroline Chisholm from the five dollar note (in favour of the Monarch) all hell broke loose. Voices ranging from feminist Anne Summers to Prime Minister Paul Keating protested. For months the new five dollar notes were defaced throughout the country at the risk of large fines.

Caroline Chisholm devoted her life to the cause of helping homeless and immigrant women settle in Australia. When she was the mother of three Caroline Chisholm began her work in Sydney in 1841. The site of her Female Immigrants' Home, granted by Governor Gipps, is marked by a plaque and I look out across Phillip Street towards it from the terrace where I work each day. It is a small memento, surrounded by the top end of town and business and professional clubs of almost exclusively male members. Most who pass the marker are unaware of it.

Single women have emigrated to Australia from the days of its earliest settlements. Most were destitute or orphaned. They began life in a rough army town with little, if any, support. Philanthropists like Caroline Chisholm and her husband Archibald pressured the governors of the colony, often in spite of bigotry and an insensitive administration, to temper

the harshness of a barracks settlement, forcing them to accept
some basic humanitarian goals. The Chisholms believed that
family life and secure employment, especially on the land,
could ease the difficulty of immigration and build a better
community.

Schemes to bring single women to Australia continued
after Caroline Chisholm. In May 1864 the Irish Emigration
Committee, for example, offered to assist 50 married couples
and 50 single women. The cost was twelve pounds for the
couples and five pounds for the single women. The continuing trickle of female immigrants coming to Australia had an
impact. In 1860, for every fourteen men in Australia there
were only ten women. By the turn of the century Australia
still had one of the highest masculinity rates in the world,
but the gap had narrowed. For every eleven men there were
now ten women. Between 1982 and 1991 unmarried women
immigrants, aged between 20 and 50, made up just over 15
per cent of all immigrants in that age group. These days
women outnumber men in Australia by at least one percentage point.

Whether Rita, Lily, Judy, Lilah, Nhung and Phi meet any
statistical averages is for others to judge. Their stories continue and are echoed elsewhere. Successful settlement is
created from more than statistics and often in spite of them.
And the stories of ordinary women migrants have rarely been
heard. These women's experiences reflect a variety of phases
and approaches to immigration in Australia, but above all
they challenge many present day views that immigrants are
a toll and a tax on the nation. They also refute a populist
image of the immigrant as a pitiful homesick non-citizen
longing for a former 'home'.

In October 1992 at The Sydney Institute, Dr James Jupp,
Director of the Centre for Immigration and Multicultural Studies at the Australian National University, evaluated Australia's
1990s approach to immigration as 'thinking small and being
frightened'. He went on to point out that Australia's humanitarian intake of immigrants was in decline and that the
immigration wave had long ago shifted from the traditions of
the 1950s of 'non-English-speaking manual workers'.
Although many who arrive to settle need development in
English language skills, Dr Jupp reminded his audience that

Australia had for many years been taking in a high proportion of immigrants who 'are better educated and skilled than the Australian average'.

James Jupp's analysis coupled well with a November 1992 report showing that Australian immigrants from new-source countries like Japan, Malaysia, South Africa, Singapore, India and Sri Lanka had considerably higher incomes than Australian-born residents.[1] At the bottom of the list, though, refugee intakes from Vietnam and Lebanon continued to record high unemployment levels.

It should be remembered however that migrant groups coming to Australia have long distinguished themselves from those going to settlements nearer home, such as the Americas. Historian Patrick O'Farrell has explained this in describing the Irish who came to Australia in the largest and earliest wave of non-English immigrants. In *The Irish in Australia* Professor O'Farrell writes that the Irish emigrant to Australia was a 'thoughtful' one, because of the distance travelled and the timing of emigrant movement to Australia. Most came during the gold rushes of the 1850s rather than because of the Irish famine a few years earlier. Moreover, the Australian immigrant needed more money:

> Of those assisted it was often alleged, then and later, that they were the scum (or dregs) of Ireland, disproportionately (because of the fact of assistance) the absolute bottom of the scale of labourers, serving girls, Catholics, and illiterates. The fact is, that even for those assisted, the journey was more expensive than that to the United States. For America it might be possible for emigrants to leave in the clothes they wore; the length of the journey to Australia, and the climatic variations, entailed the purchases of several outfits, as well as towels, utensils and incidentals.[2]

For all immigrants, in immigrant nations, earlier status is of little moment once through the quarantine check points. With a nouveau riche snobbery, locals often gain satisfaction from a superior status when measured against the newcomer. In her essay in *The Eleven Deadly Sins* Blanche d'Alpuget recalls the dilemma faced by an immigrant Polish friend: 'In Warsaw, as a young intellectual, L had been a junior member of the elite, but like poetry, status is often untranslatable. In Australia he was L Nobody'.[3]

But there is a new mood growing from the changes brought by migrants like Rita, Lily, Judy, Lilah, Nhung and Phi and 'L Nobody'. At the 'Productive Diversity in Business' conference held in Melbourne in October 1992, Paul Keating said that it was time to 'take advantage of the potentially huge national economic asset which multiculturalism represents . . . the harvest on the crop sown and nurtured by our immigration and multicultural policies'. His comments were endorsed by Tim Fischer, leader of the National Party, a day later.

Australia is now a multilingual society. As Louis de Paor told *The Australian Magazine* for 9 January 1993, 'Writing in Irish in Australia sometimes seems a more natural act than it is in Ireland. You hear so many different languages here, and they are all spoken unselfconsciously'.[4]

What all these stories demonstrate is that Australian citizens are rapidly becoming, in Maxine Hong Kingston's sense, citizens of the world. And any assessment of Australia's identity must take account of this. But more than that. It must also take account of an immigrant citizen who, without any touch of irony, says that she is lucky.

Notes

Introduction

1 Quoted in Best, B. 'Immigrant Challenge for Catholic Church', *The Age* 22 July 1980
2 Jupp, J. *Immigration* p. 81
3 Galbally, F. (Chair) 1978 *Migrant Services and Programs* AGPS, Canberra
4 Chipman, L. in 'Letters to The Editor', *The Australian* 15 July 1980
5 Hywood, G. 'An American lesson for Howard: time soothes immigration tensions', *The Australian Financial Review* 4 August 1988
6 Quoted in Herd, J. 'In Search of the Global Citizen', *The Herald* 8 September 1989

Rita

1 Gullett, H. *Unguarded Australia* p. 6
2 Jupp, J. *Immigration* p. 70

Lily

1 Kingston, M.H. *China Men* p. 55
2 May, C. *Topsawyers: The Chinese in Cairns* p. 160
3 Chang, J. *Wild Swans* p. 122
4 Quoted in Markus, A. *Fear and Hatred* p. 176
5 Stephenson, P. *The Foundations of Culture in Australia* p. 149
6 Quoted in Jupp, J. *Arrivals and Departures* p. 5
7 Lever-Tracey, C., Ip, D. et al *Asian Entrepreneurs in Australia* p. 122
8 Horne, D. (ed.) *The Coming Republic* p. 79

Judy

1 Anderson, J. *The Impersonators* p. 82
2 Quoted in Chenery, S. 'Lord's view of hell on earth', *The Australian* (*The Weekend Review*) 22–23 August 1992
3 Dow, H. (ed.) *Memories of Melbourne University* p. 179
4 Riemer, A. *Inside Outside: Life between Two Worlds* p. 161

Lilah

1 Darwent, D. 'A Great Inheritance', *Country Homes and Interiors* February 1990, p. 70
2 Gullett, H. *Unguarded Australia* p. 11
3 Sherington, G. *Australia's Immigrants* p. 98
4 Lowenstein, W. and Loh, M. *The Immigrants* p. 123

Nhung and Phi

1 Whitlam, G. 'Vietnam and her neighbours', *The National Times* 17 November 1979, p. 9
2 Quoted in Pateshall, H. 'Racism simmering in WA', *Bulletin* 4 July 1978, p. 20
3 Quoted in Grant, *The Boat People* p. 107
4 Shawcross, W. 'Sinking The Boat People', *Spectator* 3 June 1989, p. 9
5 Quoted in Dean, A. and Chater, J. 'Chinatown rebuffs the Ron Casey concept', *Sydney Morning Herald* 22 October 1987, p. 15
6 Nguyen, C. 'The Vietnamese Community: Facing a New Wave of Discrimination', *Without Prejudice* pp. 51–2
7 Quinlan, M. and Lever-Tracey, C. 'From Labour Market Exclusion to Industrial Solidarity', *Australia and Immigration— able to grow?* p. 38
8 Winton, T. *Scission* p. 106

Epilogue

1 Donovan, J. et al (eds) 1992 *Immigrants in Australia: A Health Profile* AGPS, Canberra
2 O'Farrell, P. *The Irish in Australia* pp. 64–5
3 d'Alpuget, B. 'Lust', *The Eleven Deadly Sins* p. 109
4 Quoted in Tatham, P. 'All in the clan', *The Australian Magazine* 9 January 1993, p. 19

Sources mentioned in the text

Amis, M. 1992, *Time's Arrow*, Penguin, London

Anderson, J. 1982, *The Impersonators*, Penguin, Australia

Castles, S. et al (eds) 1992, *Australia's Italians: culture and community in a changing society*, Allen & Unwin, Sydney

Chang, J. 1991, *Wild Swans: Three Daughters of China*, HarperCollins, London

d'Alpuget, B. 1981, *Turtle Beach*, Penguin, Australia

Dow, H. (cd.) 1983, *Memories of Melbourne University*, Hutchison of Australia, Melbourne

Easson, M. (ed.) 1990, *Australia and Immigration—able to grow?*, Pluto Press, Sydney

Fitzgerald, R. (ed.) 1993, *The Eleven Deadly Sins*, Heinemann, Australia

Grant, B. 1979, *The Boat People: An Age Investigation*, Penguin Australia

Gullett, H.S. 1919, *Unguarded Australia—A Plea for Immigration*, Rosebery Press, London

Haylen, L. 1959, *Chinese Journey: The Republic Revisited*, Angus & Robertson, Australia

Hemingway, E. 1977, *A Farewell to Arms*, Traid Grafton Books (HarperCollins), London

Horne, D. (ed.) 1992, *The Coming Republic*, Sun, Australia

Jupp, J. 1966, *Arrivals and Departures*, Cheshire Landsdowne, Melbourne

——1991, *Immigration*, Sydney University Press in association with Oxford University Press

Kingston, M. H. 1980, *China Men*, Picador, London

Lever-Tracey, C. and Ip, D. 1991, *Asian Entrepreneurs in Australia*, Office of Multicultural Affairs, Canberra

Lowenstein, W. and Loh, M. 1977, *The Immigrants*, Penguin, Australia

Markus, A. 1979, *Fear and Hatred*, Hale & Iremonger (Allen & Unwin), Sydney

May, C. 1984, *Topsawyers: the Chinese in Cairns 1870–1920*, James Cook University, Queensland

Nguyen, C. 1990, 'The Vietnamese community: facing a new wave of discrimination', *Without Prejudice*, no.1 September (Australian Institute of Jewish Affairs), pp. 49–54

Pascoe, R. 1987, *Buongiorno Australia: Our Italian Heritage*, Greenhouse Publications Pty Ltd, Melbourne

O'Farrell, P. 1986, *The Irish in Australia*, New South Wales University Press, Sydney

Palfreeman, A.C. 1967, *The Administration of the White Australia Policy*, Melbourne University Press, Melbourne

Riemer, A. 1992, *Inside Outside: Life Between Two Worlds*, Angus & Robertson, Australia

Sherington, G. 1990, *Australia's Immigrants*, Allen & Unwin, Sydney

Stephensen, P.R. 1936, *The Foundations of Culture in Australia*, The Forward Press, Gordon, New South Wales

Viviani, N. 1984, *The Long Journey: Vietnamese Migration and Settlement in Australia*, Melbourne University Press, Melbourne

Winton, T. 1985, *Scission*, McPhee Gribble (Penguin), Australia